HOLY CONTRADICTIONS

Holy
CONTRADICTIONS

Leslie B. Flynn

While this book is intended for profitable reading,
it is also designed for group study.
A Leader's Guide with Victor Multiuse Transparency
Masters is available from your local bookstore
or from the publisher.

VICTOR BOOKS™
A DIVISION OF SCRIPTURE PRESS PUBLICATIONS INC.
USA CANADA ENGLAND

Recommended Dewey Decimal Classification: 240
Suggested Subject Heading: BIBLICAL PARADOXES

Library of Congress Catalog Card Number: 86-63151
ISBN: 0-89693-239-7

CONTENTS

To David and Elsie Wambaugh,
good friends of many years.

ONE
OUR TOPSY-TURVY WORLD

n American who purchased a map of the world prepared in Australia was puzzled when he hung it on his office wall. It looked upside down. Australia appeared at top center, and to its left loomed South America positioned over Central America, which slanted down into the U.S.A. To Australia's lower right were the vast areas of Europe and Asia, and to the far right, Africa. This is how people from "down under" view the world.

All too often, in a somewhat similar fashion, we as "down-under" earthlings view values oppositely from the kingdom up above. This world says, "Get all you can, and can all you get." The heavenly kingdom replies, "Give, and it shall be given you."

Earth philosophizes, "Live it up. You pass this way but once." Heaven echoes back, "Only one life; 'twill soon be past. Only what's done for Christ will last."

Human nature cries, "Might is right." A higher logic answers, "Blessed are the meek, for they shall inherit the earth."

In an experiment involving people wearing special prismatic glasses, objects appeared upside down. Straight lines seemed curved. Sharp outlines appeared fringed with color. At the Fall as recorded in Genesis, man's intellect was darkened and his moral values distorted. Interestingly, in the experiment the inverted countryside, with its twisted shapes and tinted rims, slowly righted itself in a few days, all because the human brain is able to overcome the false data fed by prismatic lenses. But the sinful human heart has continued since the Fall to reverse values, producing a host of ethical illusions. Things aren't what they seem. The Prophet Isaiah warns those "who call evil good, and good evil; who substitute darkness for light and light for darkness" (Isa. 5:20, NASB). Among the horrors of totalitarianism depicted in George Orwell's *Nineteen Eighty-four* are the deceptions created through falsification of facts, which virtually deny the existence of reality. Reversal of values are reflected in three Party slogans: "War Is Peace," "Freedom Is Slavery," "Ignorance Is Strength" (Penguin Books, Ltd., 1949).

Upheaval in Beliefs and Values
Dr. Carl Henry says, "The most sudden and sweeping upheaval in beliefs and values has taken place in this century. No generation in the history of human thought has seen such swift and radical inversion of ideas and ideals as in our lifetime" (*The Christian Mindset in a Secular Society*, Multnomah, 1984, p. 81).

Henry points out that at the outset of our century courses in major Western universities frequently mentioned the God of the Bible, gave emphasis to the Ten Commandments and the Sermon on the Mount, upheld Jesus as the perfect example of morality, and spoke of the divine change required to overcome the evil propensities in man's inner disposition. But by the late 1920s a striking shift of perspective had occurred, so that no longer references focused on the God of the Bible. Rather, American education had forsaken the concept of God as the central factor in learning. Morals were considered independently of biblical basis. No longer was the new birth held necessary.

Today, no significant place remains for God in most college and university courses, except in Literature Departments where theological topics are handled in a literary context. Henry calls moral values "pale ghosts of the campus." Sometimes reliance on law and order gives way to a revolutionary approach, including violence as the method of social change.

Says Henry in *The Christian Mindset*, "The drift of 20th-century learning can be succinctly summarized in one statement: Instead of recognizing Yahweh as the source and stimulator of truth and the good, contemporary thought reduces all reality to impersonal forces and events, and insists that man himself creatively imposes upon the cosmos and upon history the only values they will ever bear" (p. 84). Such thinking provides no basis for moral imperatives. Stephen Muller, president of John Hopkins, suggests in the same book that universities may be producing a generation of "highly skilled barbarians" (p. 93). At any rate, earthly values have come recently to differ even more radically from heaven's standards.

How Values Differ
A church bulletin carried the following item:

● If a boy gets up at 4 A.M. to deliver newspapers, people say he is a go-getter. But if the church were to ask the same boy to get up a little early to deliver some handbills to announce special meetings at the church, people would say, "That's asking too much of the boy."

● If a woman spends eight hours a day away from her home working in an office, she is called an energetic wife. If, however, she is willing to do the same thing for the Lord, they say, "Religion has gone to her head."

- If a person ties himself down to make payments of $20 weekly for some luxury item for personal enjoyment, he pays willingly. But if that same person places $20 in the collection plate each week, many people would say he is out of his mind.
- If a person shouts at a football game, he is a fan. But if he gets excited about Christianity, they call him a fanatic.
- The same church member who yells like a Comanche Indian at a ball game on Saturday sits like a wooden Indian in church on Sunday. This is indeed a strange world where first things come last and last things come first.

I recall attending a Big Ten football game between Michigan State and Illinois one cold November afternoon. I was bundled up, wearing a hat that covered my ears, a fur-lined jacket, fur gloves, thermal underwear, blankets around my feet, and drinking hot cocoa from a thermos. Snow remained on the seat and under my feet. Yet 33,000 people braved the elements and sat in that stadium. I wondered how many would go to church the next morning if they had to bundle up like that, and sit in below freezing conditions in a church sanctuary. Frequently that day at the football game I heard people say, "We must be out of our minds to come here today."

Before the game I met a man who hadn't missed a Michigan State game in twelve years whether at home or away. The year before, he had suffered a broken leg during a game when players smashed into the sidelines where he was sitting. At the next game he watched from a wheelchair on the sidelines. I wondered how many would insist on going to church in a wheelchair to maintain their attendance record.

If you study philosophy or science, you're enlightened, but if you study the Bible, you're odd. If you talk about God on Monday as you do on Sunday, you're too religious.

In fact, a book published in France in 1908, *La Folie de Jesus* (*The Insanity of Jesus*), claimed that in 19th-century Europe Jesus would have been put under restraint as a megalomaniac afflicted with mystical hallucinations of a kind well known to clinical medicine. Some modern thinkers consider themselves wise, and Jesus insane. But in reality, the world with its mixed-up beliefs and behavior is on a crash course with ever-increasing momentum, hurtling toward incineration and extinction in a pile of dust.

Often today those who live it up and break moral laws are considered normal, whereas those who toe the line morally are regarded as prudes. A psychiatrist on his regular Monday morning rounds in a rest hospital for battle-fatigued soldiers visited the section where patients were about ready for discharge. As the story goes, he asked one fellow, "What did you do on your weekend pass?" Came the answer, "I gambled, drank, and caroused the whole time." The psychiatrist replied, "I think you're ready to go home."

Then the doctor approached a Christian soldier and asked what he had done over the weekend. He answered, "Oh, I stayed here much of the time. Saturday I read a few chapters from the Bible and finished a good book. Sunday I went to church morning and evening, and in the afternoon wrote my wife a letter." The psychiatrist responded, "You need to stay thirty days longer."

When Paul presented the case for the Gospel before Governor Agrippa, another Roman official, Felix, interrupted with a loud voice, "You are out of your mind, Paul! Your great learning is driving you insane" (Acts 26:24, NIV). If Felix had the opportunity today, doubtless he would change places with Paul, for with his corrected vision of reality he would see Paul as the wise man and himself as the fool.

A man walked down a street carrying a sandwich board with a message on the front. People snickered as they read, "I am a fool for Christ's sake." But as he passed, they sobered when they read the message on the back, "Whose fool are you?"

What Is Success?
Dr. Vernon Grounds, president-emeritus of Denver Conservative Baptist Seminary, in an insightful essay, "Faith for Failure," begins by clearly differentiating between worldly success and spiritual success. He suggests that worldly success can be judged from two standpoints, private experience and public impact. Privately, a man may lead a self-fulfilling life because of sufficient money for needs and luxuries; freedom from illness, depression and guilt; and ripe old age with decent burial and respect of friends.

However, a person, successful in his private sphere, may be a nobody in the eyes of those who think of success in terms of beauty (Elizabeth Taylor), sports (Dwight Gooden), wealth (Rockefeller), business (Iacocca), or intelligence (Einstein). Persons deemed successful as the world judges success often possess serious shortcomings in private life.

This spirit of using wrong standards to measure true success often infiltrates the church. Believers sometimes fall into the trap of adopting a topsy-turvy value system when they take their cues from those with mansionlike homes, lucrative incomes, foreign travel, and celebrity status. Even Christian leaders reason, "Why be a loser when you can be a winner? Adopt that program that will turn your church into a brilliant success. Why not drive a Mercedes? Why not build up your church so that it has the most beautiful sanctuary in the state? Why not be known for the biggest budget, or largest missionary giving in the denomination?"

God's standards of success differ radically from those of the world. Jesus said, "That which is highly esteemed among men is abomination in the sight of God" (Luke 16:15). Vernon Grounds in a 1977 issue of *Christianity*

12

Today asserted that "the Bible transvaluates values. . . . In other words, the Bible puts on top things that fallen man puts on bottom, and ranks last things that fallen man puts first. It praises the weakness which is strength and denounces the strength which is weakness. It praises the poverty which is wealth and denounces the wealth which is poverty. It praises the dying which is living and denounces the living which is dying. No wonder, then, that it praises the failure which is success and denounces the success which is failure. No wonder, either, that in 1 Corinthians 3:12 Paul warns us that the achievements which the world prizes as gold, silver, and precious stones God may write off as wood, hay, and stubble.

"No wonder, moreover, that when the apostle calls the roll of God's shining successes (Heb. 11), the overwhelming majority turn out to be failures as the world judges failure." Continuing, Grounds points out that many of those listed in Hebrews 11 "died as criminals—not exactly the sort of ecclesiastical dignitaries who get invited to a Presidential Prayer Breakfast."

Success, according to divine criteria laid down in 1 Corinthians 13, is not based on spellbinding pulpit oratory, depth of knowledge, accomplishments of faith, nor the numbers game, but on love without which the other items are but clanging gongs. Success is also related to service after the pattern of Jesus Christ, who came not to be waited upon but to minister as a servant. Success also issues from faithfulness to the task, even humdrum and monotonous and inconspicuous. Says Grounds in the same article, "Service inspired by love and performed in faithfulness is what constitutes success in God's eyes. . . . These are God's standards, and only God in His omniscience can use these standards in evaluating the work we do as disciples of Jesus Christ."

Senator Mark Hatfield tells of touring Calcutta with Mother Teresa and visiting the so-called "House of Dying," where sick children are cared for in their last days, and the dispensary, where the poor line up by the hundreds to receive medical attention. Watching Mother Teresa minister to these people, feeding and nursing those left by others to die, Hatfield was overwhelmed by the sheer magnitude of the suffering she and her coworkers face daily. "How can you bear the load without being crushed by it?" he asked. Mother Teresa replied, "My dear Senator, I am not called to be successful; I am called to be faithful" (*Beyond Hunger*, Art Beals, Multnomah, 1985, p. 100).

God's Strange Ways

God uses strange, unlikely, often seemingly ridiculous things to accomplish His purposes. Powerful Pharaoh was thwarted by lowly midwives who refused to drown male babies (Ex. 1:15-20). A slender rod a few feet long in Moses' hand divided the Red Sea, brought water from rock, and defeated the Amalekites (Ex. 14:16; 17:5-6; 17:9-13). Hornets drove out the Hittites (Ex. 23:28). God used a dumb donkey to get a message across to Balaam (Num. 22:28). By a mere pebble, the boy David defeated the giant Goliath (1 Sam. 17:48-52). God chooses foolish things to confound the wise, and the weak to shame the strong (1 Cor. 1:27).

God makes the wrath of men to praise Him. Chuck Colson, in prison for his part in the Watergate cover-up, thought his usefulness in life, as far as public ministry was concerned, was finished. Though he knew Christ had come into his life for a purpose, he was sure it would have nothing to do with jail. The one vow he made on his release from prison was, "Lord, I'll never go back into one of those places!" But today he heads a ministry that takes him back into prisons repeatedly, involves 30,000 volunteers across America, and annually ministers to tens of thousands of inmates and their families.

Unlikely names appear in Matthew's genealogy of Jesus. Four were women, who usually are excluded from Jewish genealogies. Some were Gentiles—in a Jewish genealogy! At least two of them were immoral, including Rahab the harlot—a person listed in Jesus' family tree! Later we find Jesus winning despised sinners like tax collectors Matthew and Zaccheus, and in His final hours forgiving the dying thief. What a turnabout when impossible prospects for salvation are converted, like Saul of Tarsus, murderous ringleader of opposition against the early church. Sinners, those improbable candidates for heaven, Jesus will receive.

Someone said, "God writes straight with crooked lines." He can accomplish His purposes by the most disjointed events or by the most out-of-the-way circumstances. God does move in mysterious ways.

Bob Pierce told the story of missionary Hubert Mitchell who wanted to bring the Gospel to the wild Kubu tribesmen in Sumatra's interior dense jungles. His main problem was not fighting his way through thick undergrowth under merciless tropical sun, but how to explain the reality of God's love to these illiterate, stone-age people. Moving bravely into a village and surrounded quickly by warriors, he sensed interest. Through an interpreter he lost no time in telling them the Gospel. As he related the account of Christ's suffering on the cross, the chief interrupted, asking, "What is cross?"

Mitchell had tribesmen cut down a small tree and strip it of its branches. Then he put two of the larger pieces together in the shape of a cross. The chief wanted to know more. "How was Christ fastened to the cross?" The missionary laid the cross on the ground and stretched himself on it. With arms outstretched, he described how soldiers had driven nails into Christ's hands and feet. The chief had still another question, "What is nail?" The villagers had never seen a nail.

Mitchell searched for something that might resemble a nail. He could find nothing. The villagers stood by watching. The chief waited, then asked more questions. The missionary felt frustrated, remembering the line from the old rhyme, "For want of a nail, the shoe was lost." Would this village never understand the love of God for want of a nail?

The dejected missionary began his evening meal of rice and fish. For dessert he picked out a can of Japanese oranges from his food supply, and absentmindedly opened it. Pouring the oranges into a dish, he was about to toss the can to a group of curious children nearby when he heard a rattling inside. Looking within, his eyes opened wide in astonishment. At the bottom of the can was a nail. Grasping the nail, the missionary rushed to the chief, who quickly gathered the villagers. Hubert Mitchell showed how the point of the nail was pounded into Christ's hands and feet. When the chief held the nail in his own hand, he realized how strong and sharp it was. The story of the cross became real to the chief and that night everyone in the village professed to receive Christ as Saviour.

Later, the chief acted as the missionary's guide on a two-week safari through the jungle so all tribesmen in the area could hear the Gospel. On the trip, the chief clutched the nail in his hand, helping the missionary explain the meaning of the cross.

The Lord says, "My thoughts are not your thoughts, neither are your ways My ways . . . for as the heavens are higher than the earth, so are My ways higher than your ways, and My thoughts than your thoughts" (Isa. 55:8-9).

Biblical Paradoxes

The Bible is replete with paradoxes. *Webster's New Collegiate Dictionary* defines *paradox* as a "statement that is seemingly contradictory, or opposed to sense, and yet is perhaps true." Dennis J. DeHaan in *Our Daily Bread* defines a biblical paradox as "an apparent contradiction that conceals a profound truth." An oxy-moron—literally "sharp dull"—is a paradoxical combination of words, such as cruel kindness, jumbo shrimp, wise fool, bittersweet, or deafening silence. A synonym for paradox is antinomy.

We do not use *paradox* as do neoorthodox theologians who try to affirm a truth while at the same time denying it. For example, such theologians sometimes deny the empty tomb, while at the same time affirming the resurrection of Christ. When you press them, you discover they do not believe His body rose, but that rather His influence lives on, or that something like faith or hope arose in the minds of His disciples because of the cross. Someone has imagined this conversation with a neo-orthodox theologian:

"Professor, do you believe in the resurrection of Jesus?"

"Of course I do. Yes, I am a believer."

"It's great to hear you say that, Professor. Some claim you're not a believer because you do not believe that Jesus rose from the dead."

"Of course, I don't believe that Jesus literally rose from the grave."

"But I thought you said you believed in the Resurrection."

"Yes, I do, but the resurrection means the rise of faith in the minds of the disciples as a result of Jesus' death on the cross."

"Oh, then you don't really believe in the Resurrection."

"Yes, of course I do!"

Such double-talk is not what we mean by biblical paradoxes. We have in mind arresting statements of divine truth that run counter to the way human nature typically thinks. Our down-under, earthly values are just the opposite to many precepts of the kingdom up above. Heavenly wisdom so often reverses earthly wisdom. Here are some principles which will be discussed in later chapters:

● Human nature likes to exalt self. But God's elevator

says that up is down, and down is up. Whoever exalts self will be abased, but whoever humbles self will be exalted.

● Impatiently, we like to hurry, even ahead of God. But in God's timetable, fast may be slow, and slow may be fast.

● Instinctively, people grab and pile up earthly treasure. But in the celestial banking system, to keep for self means ultimately losing it, whereas the unselfish person shall gain and prosper.

● By nature we live for self, but such living means loss of satisfaction. On the other hand, losing our life for Christ means finding life abundant.

● In God's number game many may turn out to be few, while little is much if God is in it.

● When it comes to the bottom-line of our real wealth, we may discover that many so-called rich are poor, and many poor of this earth are really rich.

● The worldling is sometimes miserable in the midst of his seeming joys, whereas the Christian may be joyful in the midst of his miseries.

● The strong, like Goliath, may topple. Because God's strength is made perfect in weakness, Paul could say, "When I am weak, then am I strong."

● So many people do as they please, indulging in license, and end up as slaves. The broad way leads to destruction and limitation, but he who walks the narrow way, as a slave of Jesus Christ, finds liberty and life.

● Man's cleverness may prove to be folly. However, the "foolish" ways of God prove wise.

● God's final judgment may result in a reversal of earthly status. Many prominent persons down here will be nobodies in heaven, but many unhonored down here will have front seats up there. To be chief we must be a servant.

These divine paradoxes show that the race is not always to the swift nor the battle to the strong, nor bread to the aggressive, nor riches to the wise, nor favor to the skillful. Values of the higher kingdom may seem "upside down" to the natural mind, but in reality those values will turn "downside up" the thinking and living of those who follow them. Though Paul and his missionary party were described by their opponents in Thessalonica as men who had "turned the world upside down," the divine message had in actuality created lifestyles that were now right-side up (Acts 17:6). The apostles and their company marched to a different and higher drumbeat.

Earlier, we referred to an experiment involving prismatic glasses which made objects appear upside down. Realizing that our moral views and values have been distorted by the Fall of man, we need not only the regenerating power of the new birth, but also the continuous enlightenment of the Holy Spirit to help us see as God sees.

Correct my vision, Father,
Awry and warped by sin,
That through Your Spirit's blessing,
Your truth may shine again.
—H.G.B. in *Our Daily Bread,* 8/28/85

TWO
GOD'S ELEVATOR

Up is down.
Down is up.

woman buying fluffy, feathery stuffing for a pillow and hearing the price exclaimed, "That's expensive! The price has gone up!" The clerk replied, "That's right—down is up."

These words, spoken in a business context, also echo a spiritual paradox stated repeatedly throughout Scripture. For example: "Before his downfall a man's heart is proud, but humility comes before honor" (Prov. 18:12). Other related references include Proverbs 11:2; 29:23; Ezekiel 17:24; James 4:6, 10.

Worldly propaganda shouts, "Toot your own horn. He that tooteth not his own horn, verily it shall not be tooted." However, the heavenly kingdom cautions, "Let another man praise thee, and not thine own mouth" (Prov. 27:2). Pondering her low estate, Mary said in her Magnificat, "He hath put down the mighty from their seats, and exalted them of low degree" (Luke 1:52). Jesus warned, "Whosoever shall exalt himself shall be abased; and he that shall humble himself shall be exalted" (Matt. 23:12). *Exalt* is related to a noun which means *height*. Jesus gave this warning because some Pharisees were seeking the high seats at feasts and synagogues, high honors through religious garb and ostentatious works, and high titles addressed to them in the marketplace. They would discover that, in God's elevator, heights can lead to depths.

UP IS DOWN

In God's economy, pride is an attitude that He abhors. The proud person congratulates himself for his accomplishments—for being who he is. Here are some errors of self-exaltation:

Pride overestimates self. Self-exaltation causes a person to ascribe to himself an importance and reputation which he knows is false but which, nevertheless, he wants others to accept. Vainglory wants people to notice, admire, flatter. High heels were invented by King Louis XIV of France, who, shorter than most men, ordered shoes made with heels that added several spurious inches to his height.

Pride leads people to strut cockily across the pages of history, seeing self as accomplishing great things because of "*my* initiative, *my* ingenuity, *my* industry," often openly trumpeting their own praises. But Proverbs 27:2 says, "Let another man praise thee, and not thine own mouth; a stranger, and not thine own lips."

A man remarked that the only time he remembered that he was seriously tempted to stretch the truth was when it inflated his personal status. How easy, for example, to overbask in the limelight of your part in the school play, your position on the varsity team, an honorary degree, or a new title given you by your company. How easy to exaggerate salary, education, and achievements. When Jesus was tempted to display His power by jumping off the temple pinnacle without injury, He resisted such self-exaltation.

Pride looks down on others. C.S. Lewis suggested that each person's pride is in competition with everyone else's pride. Delight comes not so much from being smart, wealthy, or good-looking, but from having more of it than your neighbor. When a person is loaded with money, the tendency is to look down on those with less. But God hates "a proud look" (Prov. 6:17).

Pride stabs at God. A man who had just agreed to teach an adult Sunday School class nervously paced the floor the night before his lesson. "I'm not worthy of this sacred trust," he told his wife. "I feel so unworthy of trying to show people how to live a better life."

His wife answered, "Just remember you are only going to tell about God, not *be* God!"

Pride may make a man an unbearable snob, alienating family and friends. Some people even get themselves confused with God through pride. Benjamin Disraeli was once described as a self-made man who worshiped his creator. Exalted self-exaltation which looks smugly at others heads toward self-deification. Pride rejects God's sovereignty over our lives, rebels against His laws and limits, would rob Him of His glory, and if possible topple Him from His throne. Lucifer wanted to be like God (Isa. 14:13-14). So did our first parents (Gen. 3:5). Also the coming Antichrist "shall magnify himself above all" (Dan. 11:37). He too will tumble.

Pride can trip you after you reach success in later life. A.W. Pink, respected Bible teacher of yesteryear, said: "It is striking to observe that Scripture records not a single instance of a young saint disgracing his profession. Recall the histories of young Joseph; the Hebrew maid in Naaman's household; David as a stripling engaging Goliath; Daniel's early days and his three youthful companions in the furnace; and it will be found that all of them quitted themselves nobly. On the other hand, there are numerous examples where men in middle life and of gray hairs grievously dishonored their Lord." He points out that young Christians sense their feebleness, but "some older Christians seem far less conscious of their danger, and so God often suffers them to have a fall, that He may stain the pride of their self-glory, and that others may see it is nothing in the flesh—standing, rank, age, or attainments—which insures our safety, but that He upholds the humble and casts down the proud" (*Exposition of Hebrews,* Baker, p. 957).

Moses committed the sin of presumption at the end of the wilderness journey. David fell into his sin of adultery in the prime of life and after he had become king. When anointed king at the start of his career, Saul remarked, "Am not I a Benjamite, of the smallest of the tribes of Israel?" (1 Sam. 9:21) But after many victories, the humble king grew haughty, broke the laws of God, and at his death evoked this exclamation, "How are the mighty fallen!" (2 Sam. 1:19) After the miraculous destruction of his powerful enemy Sennacherib, Hezekiah "was magnified in the sight of all nations," and "his heart was lifted up" (2 Chron. 32:23, 25). When Babylonian ambassadors visited him, he made the mistake of displaying all the treasures of his storehouse. Because of Hezekiah's boastful ostentation, the Prophet Isaiah told him that all those treasures would be carried to Babylon (2 Kings 20:12-19).

One can only admire Dr. Charles E. Blair, pastor of Calvary Temple in Denver, for his honest confession in the book *The Man Who Could Do No Wrong.* His 2,300-capacity auditorium often overflowed at all three Sunday services. The blurb on the back cover says, "He grew up on the wrong side of the tracks. He built one of the largest churches in America. Then he made a mistake." One day the newspapers carried the humiliating headline, "Blair indicted: Pastor, fund-raiser accused of fraud." Charged with 21 counts of fraudulent practices in the sale of church securities, he faced the possibility of a $100,000 fine, plus up to 60 years in the penitentiary.

When Blair was fingerprinted, the clerk, placing one of the minister's hands in the ink, said: "Twenty years ago I was driving my car listening to your radio show, Dr. Blair. I pulled over to the side of the road and surrendered my life to Jesus. I never dreamed I'd be taking the fingerprints of the same preacher."

Found guilty, Blair was fined $12,750 and placed on five years' probation. Still pastor of this thriving church, Blair in the book outlines lessons he learned and suggests ways to avoid ego trips.

The foreword speaks of "success beyond his wildest dreams to public humiliation. Charles came to stand in our minds for every one of us caught in the trap of his own image. Needing to appear successful, wise, happy—allowing ourselves no room for failure" (*The Man Who Could Do No Wrong,* John and Elizabeth Sherrill, Chosen Books).

"Thus saith the Lord, 'Let not the wise man glory in his wisdom, neither let the mighty man glory in his might, let not the rich man glory in his riches, but let him that glorieth glory in this, that he understandeth and knoweth Me, that I am the Lord which exercises loving-kindness, judgment, and righteousness in the earth; for in these things I delight,' saith the Lord" (Jer. 9:23-24).

Overconfidence may result in carelessness. "Pride goeth before destruction, and an haughty spirit before a fall" (Prov. 16:18). A king of Israel once said to Ben-Hadad, cocky king of Syria, "One who puts on his armor should not boast like one who takes it off" (1 Kings 20:11, NIV). Ben-Hadad suffered defeat in the ensuing battle.

A championship team rests on its laurels, eases up on practice, forgets to hustle, and loses the game.

A big boy, cocksure he will win the 100-yard dash at the Sunday School picnic, comes in behind a small and younger lad whom he had previously disdained. "Seest thou a man wise in his own conceit? There is more hope of a fool than of him" (Prov. 26:12).

As a man walks proudly around the ballroom of a large hotel in his brand-new suit, a protruding nail rips a jagged tear in his sleeve.

I gloated to my wife about my choice of exercise, a stationary bike, which I could ride indoors regardless of pelting rain or blowing snow; it permitted me to watch TV or read, and even take my pulse while pedaling. Her form of exercise, walking, meant enduring all types of unpleasant weather, no TV, and difficulty in pulse taking. One day I developed an abdominal strain. The doctor told me to stop my biking and switch to—you guessed it—walking!

The proud person forgets the fickleness of the crowd. An athlete may ride the crest of fame for a time but he may soon be forgotten. Stars fade and new ones loom on the horizon—for a while.

The overconfident person forgets his weaknesses. Peter and all the disciples asserted that they would not deny Jesus. They failed their word. The Bible warns, "Wherefore let him that thinketh he standeth take heed lest he fall" (1 Cor. 10:12).

Overconfidence invites others to deflate that arrogance. Because of vanity, a perennial swindle called the "puff sheet" racket has thrived. The promoter of the puff sheet scans newspapers and business reports from all over the country looking for job promotions or formations of new partnerships or companies. He rewrites an item, packing it with lavish praise, then reads it over the phone to the unsuspecting victim, representing himself as the editor of an important sounding business publication with a name perhaps closely resembling *The Wall Street Journal.* The caller asks for an immediate OK since the issue is going to press within the hour. Unable to withstand the flattery, the victim readily complies with the request to buy a sizable quantity at the "bargain" rate of 35 cents each. Receiving his copies, the victim soon discovers that the business journal is nothing but a skimpy, cheap pamphlet. His pride has duped him!

Stuffed shirts who vaunt their superior position, power, possessions, prestige, or performance become targets of the inferior, provoking others to stick a pin in their balloon to deflate their ego. Uneasy lies the haughty head that wears the crown. When you boast that you're king of the castle, others will surely try to dislodge you from your place of preeminence. A high tree attracts the wind.

Every great empire, gloating in its might, has been displaced by some other empire. Kipling wrote "Recessional" with its repetitive "lest we forget" to remind Great Britain not to exploit others, warning that its vaunted empire could crumble into dust.

Jesus told a parable of those who took the best seats at dinners but who were demoted to inferior places when more honorable guests arrived (Luke 14:7-11). When King David was near death, his son, Adonijah, exalted himself, saying, "I will be king," and prepared to usurp the throne. But David, hearing this, proclaimed Solomon king. Adonijah had to flee for his life (1 Kings 1). Says the wise man, "Stand not in the place of great men, for better it is that it be said unto thee, 'Come up hither,' than that thou shouldest be put lower" (Prov. 25:6-7).

Two seminary students were scheduled to deliver 12-minute sermons in the homiletics class. The student assigned the second sermon was a braggadocia who through-out the school year had proclaimed himself an accomplished preacher. On the morning of the class, the first fellow, quiet and unassuming, gave an impressive talk, showing thorough research and complete mastery of his material. When the second student stood to start his sermon, it was evident that the quality of the first sermon had intimidated him, and also that he had not prepared well. After a few faltering sentences, he put his head on the pulpit and announced he could not go on. Needless to say, he was deeply humiliated.

Abasement may come through carelessness engendered by exaggerated self-confidence, or by cockiness which invites others to poke at us. Or God may cause us to tumble.

Overconfidence displeases God. The previous causes listed for a person's humiliation are natural outworkings, but this one has a supernatural basis. "Everyone who is proud in heart is an abomination to the Lord" (Prov. 16:5). God often cuts short whatever is too highly exalted.

The Pilgrims sailing from England in 1620 reported seeing God take such action. They discovered that the Atlantic can be extremely rough late in the year. Men, women, and children were cooped up below deck for weeks. Privacy and sanitation were impossible. The tossing sea made conditions intolerable. But that wasn't all. As some of the Pilgrims lay helplessly in their confined quarters, gripped by seasickness and disease, a certain sailor delighted in tormenting them, sadistically assuring them they were about to die, and what a pleasure he would have in tossing them overboard. Suddenly this sailor himself took violently ill, died within a day, and was thrown overboard. The Pilgrims viewed his death as a judgment from God.

God cast down ambitious Lucifer (Isa. 14:12-15). When men of Babel built a tower to reach heaven and make a name for themselves, God confused their language and scattered them over the earth (Gen. 11:1-9). When Korah led a revolt of 250 princes against Moses and Aaron, God opened up the ground and swallowed these rebels who had lifted themselves up against God's chosen leaders (Num. 16:1-35).

When Sennacherib, king of Assyria, sought to terrify the defenders of Jerusalem with his pompous boast of power and supremacy, the Lord spoke through the Prophet Isaiah, "Because you have raged against Me and your arrogance has come into My ears, I will put My hook in your nose and My bit in your mouth, and I will turn you back on the way by which you came" (2 Kings 19:28, RSV). God's angel smote the entire Assyrian army in one night. Soon after, Sennacherib was slain by his sons.

Nebuchadnezzar, king of Babylon, walking in his palace, boasted with arrogant egocentricity, "Is not this great Babylon I have built . . . by my mighty power and for the glory of my majesty?" (Dan. 4:30, NIV) With the words "still on his lips," a heavenly voice told him that his kingdom had departed from him, and that he would behave like an animal. Nebuchadnezzar's hair grew as long as eagles' feathers, and his nails like the claws of a bird. Scholars believe he suffered the animal-like psychosis, lycanthropy.

Though knowing all this, his son Belshazzar lifted up his heart against God, making sacrilege of the holy vessels captured from Jerusalem (Dan. 5:22-23). Then the handwriting on the wall told him his number was up. That night he was slain and his kingdom toppled!

For King Uzziah successes came rapidly. Jerusalem's walls were strengthened. Military outposts were established. Cisterns were built for rain storage. Prosperity, unparalleled since Solomon's time, prevailed. Then Uzziah's heart lifted up in pride. Usurping priestly function, he pressed into the holy place, a censer in hand. But before the usurper could scatter incense, white spots of leprosy appeared on his forehead. Shoved out by the priests, he remained a victim of leprosy for life, living in enforced privacy and removed from government work (2 Chron. 26:16-21).

King Herod, grandson of Herod the Great, sat on a throne in Caesarea, and made an oration to which the people responded with a shout, " 'It is the voice of a god, and not of a man.' And immediately the angel of the Lord smote him, because he gave not God the glory; and he ... gave up the ghost" in great physical agony (Acts 12:22-23).

During Hitler's regime in Germany, parents in the Third Reich were required to teach a table grace to their small children: "Führer, my Führer, sent to me from God, protect and maintain me throughout my life. Thou hast saved Germany from the deepest need. I thank thee today for my daily bread. Remain at my side and never leave me, Führer, my Führer, my faith, my light. Heil, Mein Führer!" (Joseph J. Carr, *The Twisted Cross,* Huntington House, 1985, p. 39).

Auto entrepreneur John Z. DeLorean, reflecting on the failure of his sports car company, a cocaine conspiracy trial, and divorce from his model wife, said: "I believe I deserve what happened to me. The deadliest sin is pride. I was an arrogant egomaniac. I needed this, as difficult as it was, to get my perspective back" (*Rockland County Journal News*, 9/21/85).

Now we turn from the abasement of the proud to the exaltation of the humble.

DOWN IS UP

As surely as the person who puffs self will be ultimately deflated, so the one who abases self will be surely exalted. In the divine kingdom, as up leads to down, so down leads to up. By taking a lower seat we can be more easily invited to a higher, more noble spot. If we do not blow our own trumpet, the quietness may permit others to more readily recognize our abilities. Above all, we have the promise of God to lift the lowly. Proverbs says, "Before honor is humility" (15:33).

Dr. R.A. Torrey spoke on "Seven Reasons Why God Used D.L. Moody." One was Moody's humility. Torrey commented that he had known many promising young ministers, whom as time went on, God had to lay aside because they became vain over their ministry.

Sold into Egypt, Joseph humbled himself first as a slave in Potiphar's house, and later, falsely accused, as a prisoner in Pharaoh's dungeon. In both situations he was made overseer. After 13 years of humble servitude, Joseph was elevated to second-in-command over all Egypt.

Just before David battled Goliath, he told King Saul of two occasions when, as a shepherd-boy, he had rescued a lamb from wild animals. He gave God the credit, "The Lord who delivered me from the paw of the lion and the paw of the bear will deliver me from the hand of this Philistine" (1 Sam. 17:37, NIV). When Goliath boasted disdainfully how he would give the youth's flesh to the birds, David humbly replied, "This day will the Lord deliver thee into mine hand" (vv. 42-46).

When David encouraged the people to build a temple, he praised, "Thine, O Lord, is the greatness, and the power, and the glory, and the victory, and the majesty: for all that is in the heaven and in the earth is Thine; Thine is the kingdom, O Lord, and Thou are exalted as head above all" (1 Chron. 29:11). No wonder David had been lifted to be king over Israel to reign 40 years, defeat his enemies, and be head over many nations.

A supreme example of exaltation through abasement is Jesus Christ, who despite being God, became man, a servant of no reputation, and died the ignominious death reserved for aliens, slaves, and criminals. Because of this condescension God highly exalted Him, giving Him a name above every name (Phil. 2:5-11).

How to Prevent Self-Exaltation

Three principles relating to self, others, and God will help prevent excessive pride. They are:

● *A proper estimate of ourselves and our abilities.* First of all, we need to see the weakness and depravity of our old nature. Harold L. Myra, president of Christianity Today, Inc., in *Leadership* magazine says that "a realistic view of our exceeding sinfulness and frailty is an extremely positive, energizing, healthy perspective. . . . When we see the full truth about ourselves, we are freed from the agony of worrying about others' evaluation." This understanding of our true condition releases the believer into the grace of God. Seeing God accepts us in Christ, we accept ourselves. Myra quotes Thomas a Kempis, " 'No one is richer than he, no one more potent, no one more free, who knows how to abandon self and reckon himself the lowliest' " (*Imitation of Christ,* p. 8).

The resultant, legitimate self-esteem is necessary for a healthy self-image. Downgrading self in mock humility like *David Copperfield's* Uriah Heep is undesirable, as is an overestimate of our self-worth. Paul tells each "not to think of himself more highly than he ought to think, but to think soberly, according as God hath dealt to every man the measure of faith" (Rom. 12:3).

If we fulfill whatever authority God has given us with gratitude, commitment, and accountability, whether as parent, teacher, manager, foreman, or elected office holder, we will escape the pitfall of power.

Since arrogance involves a bloated and dishonest self-evaluation, a proper estimate of our abilities and responsibilities will do much to forestall self-exaltation. Says a Chinese proverb, "Who flies not high falls not low."

● *Regard for others' worth.* George Whitefield's anointed ministry in 18th-century England brought instant fame, so that he almost always preached to crowded congregations. Outdoor throngs of 20,000 were common with everyone able to hear his majestic voice. Instead of reacting with pride, but realizing the gifts and service of all believers are necessary for the success of the Lord's work, he usually signed his letters, "Less than the least of all saints. George Whitefield."

Principal Cairns, headmaster of an English school, as a member of a group assigned to sit at the front of a large gathering, walked onto the platform in a line with the other dignitaries. When his turn came to step through the door, his appearance was met by a burst of applause. Immediately Cairns stepped back to let the man behind pass him, then began to applaud his colleague. In his modesty he assumed the applause was for another.

When Billy Graham visited Ireland, he determined to walk down a main street of a religiously divided city with Arthur Blesset, the man known as the cross-carrying Christian. The dividing line between warring Catholic and Protestant factions, this street was often the scene of death by bullets shot from nearby houses. As the marchers sat in a car to pray before the walk, Billy Graham turned to the young man who had arranged Blesset's tour. "I need all the advice you can give me before we start this walk. You're going to have to treat me as a student of personal evangelism," he said. "I don't consider myself as possessing the gift of dealing with one individual." And that from the world-famous evangelist who for decades had addressed thousands of people night after night in large crusades.

Paul wrote, "Let nothing be done through strife or vainglory, but in lowliness of mind let each esteem other better than themselves" (Phil. 2:3). It's remarkable how much can be accomplished for the Lord when we don't care who gets the credit.

● *Recognition that glory belongs to God.* Often the Christian public treats successful writers, singers, and TV preachers as superstars. Writing in *Eternity* magazine, Joseph Bayly warned that "the eminently successful Christian may begin to believe the publicity that's written about him/her [and] may come to have a bloated opinion of his importance as a result of being interviewed, having his picture on magazine covers, being adulated by a fan club that hangs on his every word and accepts his every action" (Sept. 1985, p. 88).

It's particularly difficult for a new believer to cope with superstardom status. This is why the Lord put this qualification on church leadership: "He must not be a recent convert, or he may become conceited and fall under the same judgment as the devil" (1 Tim. 3:6, NIV).

The Lord says, "My glory will I not give to another" (Isa. 42:8). How does this divine prohibition stack up with today's practice of applauding singers and speakers in church after an excellent presentation? One discerning believer suggested that it depends on what goes on in the heart of the applauder. If it's merely adulation for a human being, then it's wrong. But sometimes it's a way of saying amen to the truth contained in the performance. Likely, many are expressing appreciation for the dedication of abilities which made for the skillful performance. If it's permissible for a preacher or emcee to use his voice to express appreciation after a concert, why isn't it acceptable for an audience to applaud to show its commendation? Hopefully, many clap to praise God for what they have just heard.

Performers must not let themselves be carried away with the applause but rather should give God the credit. When the English scholar-pastor Michael Green finished a lecture at Asbury Seminary, the students gave him a standing ovation. Somewhat embarrassed, he rose to his feet, began to clap, then while still clapping, lifted his hands upward. He wanted God to get the glory.

Jesus taught, "Blessed are the poor in spirit, for theirs is the kingdom of heaven" (Matt. 5:3). He also taught that to inherit the kingdom we first have to humble ourselves as a little child (Matt. 18:1-4).

When the aged Emperor Francis Joseph of Austria-Hungary, who had ruled for more than 60 years, died during World War I, according to tradition he was carried to the gates of the crypt of the Church of the Capuchins in Vienna. When the procession knocked on the gate, a voice from within called out, "Who is there?" Back came the answer, "His Serene Majesty, the Emperor of Austria."

The voice within replied, "I know him not. Who is there?" Again the answer came back, "The Apostolic King of Hungary."

Once more the voice within cried out, "I know him not. Who is there?" This time the answer came back, "Our brother, Francis Joseph, a sinner."

This time the gates opened, and the emperor was laid among his ancestors.

We need to be constantly on guard against too high an opinion of ourselves and our abilities. We need to ever look around at others and recognize their talents and dedication. Above all, we should always recall that God deserves all the glory for whatever happens to or through us.

THREE
DIVINE TIMETABLE

Fast is slow.
Slow is fast.

We live in an age of speed. Cars waiting for the light to change poise like rockets on the launching pad. Elevators that stop at every floor tax our patience. We must have the express subway, not the local. Often we even walk up the escalator. Jets fly the Atlantic so quickly, that it's possible to get mugged in London and New York on the same day.

But what seems to be speedy may turn out slow, and what seems delayed may turn out fast. The car that catapults from the corner may be stopped by another red light or by a turning truck or by a traffic problem, while a slower-starting vehicle may overtake and pass the impatient driver. Something like the fable of the tortoise and the hare.

While most of the nation is on daylight saving time each summer, several counties in Indiana (at last report) do not comply. Though one town's post office advances its clocks, its only mail carrier sticks with standard time. The local radio station observes fast time while the local newspaper refuses to budge from slow time. One of the two drugstores moves the clock ahead, and the other leaves it back.

The county sheriff is on daylight; the county courthouse is on standard. Fast is slow and slow is fast.

Scientific devices can slow down or speed up time. Expanding time considerably, a special camera reduces a continuous flow of milk to a set of individual, separate drops. In the other direction, by means of a time-lapse camera, an entire Rose Bowl football game, including the half-time show, is compressed to a total of 35 seconds. In the Lord's sight one day is as a thousand years, and a thousand years as one day (2 Peter 3:8).

Picture two men coming to Jesus in His carpenter days, each asking help in the building of his house. One selects a spot far away from a cliff where it's hard to dig, but near the sandy riverbed which was dry most of the year. Jesus warns, "Build on a rocky foundation, even though it takes time. When the storms come and the stream swells, you'll be sorry if you take the fast way and build on the sand." But he disregards Jesus' advice. However, the other man resists the shortcut approach and builds on rock, demanding struggle, energy, and time. Jesus ended His Sermon on the Mount with the story of two such men, one of whom discovered a principle of the upside-down kingdom the hard way. When the rains destroyed the hastily improvised lodging, the first builder learned that fast is slow. When the second home stood, that builder experienced the truth that slow is fast.

FAST IS SLOW

A few years ago a Navy jet fighter shot itself down over a Nevada desert while testing a new cannon mounted on its wing. The plane was flying at supersonic speed, but the cannon shells were subsonic. The fighter actually ran into the shells it had fired seconds before. The jet was traveling too fast for its own good.

Other examples. A driver in a hurry races a train to the crossing and is hit broadside. A young man quits high school to take a job, but after a few futile years of trying to rise in his company, he discovers the need for more education, so goes back to school. Starry-eyed teenagers marry too soon and suffer through several rough years which could have been avoided had they waited. A woman rushes the grief process after the death of a loved one by stoically repressing her tears, and experiences prolonged emotional stress before emerging into normalcy.

We hurry through a repair task, find ourselves all thumbs, bungle the job badly, and have to do it all over again. Too soon a return to work after illness may mean another recuperation period.

Proverbs says, "An inheritance quickly gained at the beginning will not be blessed at the end" (20:21, NIV). A fast buck may lead to slow time behind prison bars, or to a period of recouping financial loss.

Proverbs also advises against rushing into an argument with your neighbor with an ill-advised or poorly prepared case, lest you become humiliated (25:8). Proverbs 29:20 goes on to warn, "Seest thou a man that is hasty in his words? There is more hope of a fool than of him." A quick retort may precipitate a quarrel, resulting in a prolonged grudge.

Bob Harris, weatherman for New York TV station WPIX-TV and the nationally syndicated Independent Network news, had to weather a public storm of his own making in 1979. Though he had studied math, physics, and geology at three colleges, he left school without a degree but with a strong desire to be a media weatherman. He phoned WCBS-TV, introducing himself as a Ph.D. in geophysics from Columbia University. The phony degree got him in the door. After a two-month tryout, he was hired as an off-camera forecaster for WCBS. For the next decade his career flourished. He became widely known as "Dr. Bob." He was also hired by the *New York Times* as a consulting meteorologist. The same year both the Long Island Railroad and then Baseball Commissioner Bowie Kuhn hired him.

Forty years of age and living his childhood dream, he found himself in public disgrace and national humiliation when an anonymous letter prompted WCBS management to investigate his academic credentials. Both the station and the *New York Times* fired him. His story got attention across the land. He was on the *Today Show*, the *Tomorrow Show*, and in *People Weekly*, among others. He thought he'd lose his home and never work in the media again. Several days later the Long Island Railroad and Bowie Kuhn announced they would not fire him. Then WNEW-TV gave him a job.

Harris, who has put the episode behind him, admits it was a dreadful mistake on his part, and doubtless played a role in his divorce. He believes there are people who will never hire him, and that he will continue to pay. Says he, "I took a shortcut that turned out to be the long way around, and one day the bill came due. I will be sorry as long as I am alive" (Nancy Shulins, AP newsfeatures writer, May 1985 in *Journal News,* Nyack, N.Y.).

Sometimes we travel too fast for our good. We are too busy to write a letter, make that phone call, remember that anniversary, visit that sick person, witness to that unbelieving friend, bake that cake for the sick neighbor, or give time to our family.

In 1985 a 23-year-old man stood trial for the grizzly, sadomasochistic murder of a Swedish youth in a town 30 miles north of New York City. For nearly an hour his mother, a New York University scientist specializing in gum diseases, gave testimony punctuated by sobs. She recounted how for almost a year she had left her infant son with her parents in the Philippines while she and her husband, a United Nations executive, pursued their careers here. "I didn't realize it would be traumatic for a baby 14 months old," she said, adding that her family regularly showed the boy photographs of her and her husband so he'd remember them. "Whatever mistakes I made, I didn't do it out of meanness. . . . We wanted to be achievers. . . . My husband is very busy. I guess we're both very busy" (*Journal News*, Nyack, N.Y., September 12, 1985).

Psychiatrist M. Robert Gomberg, executive director of Jewish Family and Community Service, warns that too many American parents are trying to raise their children at "jet speed." He cites the example of a mother who boasted of her daughter's public performance on the piano. The child was nervous and nauseous before each exhibition and tired afterward. The mother said that at each concert she herself "died a thousand deaths." She had no answer to the question, "Why do you do it?" Some parents, he comments, just want to wear their children like medals. He suggests that each individual child be allowed to develop at his or her own pace.

Bible Examples

● *Abraham and Sarah* ran ahead of God when they tried to hurry His promise of an heir. Barren and seemingly unlikely to have a baby—much less a progeny as numerous as stars and sand—Sarah suggested to Abraham to have a child by her handmaid, Hagar. Because of their impatience, Ishmael was born, a source of trouble for Abraham's offspring even until today. Had they waited, they would have discovered that slow is fast, for God in His time did give them Isaac (Gen. 16).

● *Rebekah* plotted with her favorite son, Jacob, to get the family blessing through deception. As a result he had to flee home, then spend 20 years an exile, likely never seeing his mother on earth again. Far better had Jacob waited for God to give him the blessing on His divine timetable (Gen. 27).

● *Joshua* under God's hand conquered Jericho, and the neighboring Gibeonites, thinking of their own survival, sent ambassadors pretending to be from a distant land, asking peace. Hurriedly, without asking "counsel at the mouth of the Lord," Joshua was tricked into making a league with a people God had ordered him to destroy (Josh. 9:15). Though he made them servants, they became a thorn in Israel's side for generations. Joshua found that fast is slow.

● *Asahel,* fleet-footed as a wild roe, chased General Abner till he caught up with him. Abner told him to get lost and pursue someone else. When Asahel persisted, Abner speared him. Asahel's speed led to his death (2 Sam. 2:18-23).

Busyness may be bad. By living at too fast a pace, or by trying to do too much in a limited span of time, we may merely go through the motions, or spin our wheels, or hurt our health, or not do a good job, and lose out time-wise in the end anyway.

Dr. David A. MacLennan wrote:

Busyness, even in our Lord's service, may have a more deadly result than jangled nerves, frayed tempers, and poisonous fatigue. The Church of Saint Peter can become the Church of Saint Vitus. For the communion of saints we can substitute the commotion of the saints. Instead of going about doing good we may settle for just going about. Agitation and activity, even on behalf of a program, may find us bustling on the periphery instead of digging at the center of the faith (*Resources for Sermon Preparation,* Westminster, p. 175).

A missionary on furlough boasted that he had not taken a vacation for nine years. In his tenth year, he had to take ten months off to regain his health, the period being the equivalent of his neglected annual month's vacation for ten years.

Someone commented that streamlined, high-speed living has transformed America into a civilized madhouse, and that what we need are fewer 60-mile-an-hour sports cars and more rocking chairs. Though we would not wish to retrogress to the horse-and-buggy days, a little less hurry and rush would do us all good. When it became known back in the '60s that President Kennedy liked to relax, while working, sitting in a rocking chair, orders for rocking chairs boomed in the furniture industry. A rocking-chair display in a department store was labeled "The world's oldest tranquilizer." A slower gait may be good for both physical and spiritual health.

SLOW IS FAST

Some things cannot be done in a hurry, no matter how strong the impulse to achieve instant goals. No shortcut to success exists in the various areas of life. Even personal grooming consumes time. Getting your education may slow you down but later you may climb the corporate ladder more swiftly. Growing in the Christian life requires time.

It takes time to raise a family. Said a woman to the mother of four fine grown sons, "I'd give 30 years of my life to raise four boys like yours!"

"That's exactly what it cost me!" came the reply.

It takes time to make friends. Companionship is not won overnight, but demands the expenditure of many, many hours in genuine, warm involvement with another. Friendly conversations, baby-sitting for neighbors, or running errands may prove a judicious use of time to open the door to later, God-directed witness.

It takes time to make a marriage work, develop talents, to write or read a book, conduct a scientific experiment, to learn the plays on the football team. The Good Samaritan's plans for the evening were demolished when he spent those hours giving first-aid to the mugger's victim, taking him to the inn, and nursing him through the night.

Divine providence uses delays. Though transcendent, our God does not govern our world by remote control. He is continually involved in the sustaining of the universe so that every change of the weather, every movement of the stars, and every activity of the minutest creature is directed by His all-wise providence.

Even the thwarting of our plans is in His hand. In the hour of delay and desperation we fret, "How long, O Lord?" Though delays thorn the flesh, sometimes in the divine schedule slow is fast, for the stops as well as the starts of a good man are ordered of the Lord. How often in the Bible, history, and experience God has proven Himself on time in fulfilling plans, answering prayer, relieving pain and perplexity, and supplying preparation and guidance for the future.

Partnership magazine (May-June 1985) tells of a young mother who wanted so desperately to be on the mission field. Both she and her husband had recently attained a longtime ambition by earning master's degrees. Both were headed for full-time work overseas, and anxious to get there. But necessary debt incurred in their final semester required her conscientious husband to give his employer a year of his time. So every day she watched her overqualified, highly trained, seminary-graduate husband don a plant uniform and go off to a mundane job. Sinking down in a chair behind a pile of diapers, she sighed, "This isn't what I dreamed of when we plugged our way through graduate school a few months ago." Friends had finished their preparation and had left while she and her husband still plodded on. It seemed so long till a year would be up. Also, looking around at the small two-bedroom, furnished apartment, she reminded herself that she was surrounded by someone else's furniture.

Then one day she reassessed the situation. How like Moses, who after being brought up in the wisdom of Egypt's palace, found himself tending sheep, a boring job for which he was overqualified. For 40 years he tended a flock not even his. Would he ever get to the task for which he was called? But this long interim trained him in the ways of the desert, thus preparing him to lead the Israelites through years of wilderness.

She had received a top-notch education, though not using it then. She was minding another's apartment. Still in her waiting period, she was being groomed for what lay ahead. She began to read books to help her in our complex society, and sought opportunities for current service. She saw herself as in a holding stage. A footnote to the article stated that she and her husband arrived for their first year of service in Zimbabwe with TEAM, doubtless better prepared because of the delay.

A new missionary couple to Brazil sent out a prayer letter headed *Our Schedule* with the *Our* crossed out so that it read *God's Schedule*. In one column they listed *Our Schedule* with all their projected dates for accomplishing specific goals. In the parallel column they listed the actual dates their goals were met, all much later than planned. They said that if the Lord had shown them His schedule ahead of time, they would not have wanted to believe it, and would have argued that there was an easier and better way. But at the end of their letter they listed six valuable lessons which they learned through God's timing. They prefaced their letter with a quotation from Isaiah, " 'For My thoughts are not your thoughts, neither are your ways My ways,' declares the Lord" (55:8, NIV).

Biblical Examples
● *Joseph* spent two years in prison because the butler forgot his promise to Joseph to put in a good word for him to Pharaoh, but when Pharaoh had a dream none of the wise men could explain, the butler remembered Joseph. The result—Joseph was elevated to second-in-command of all Egypt (Gen. 40–42). Joseph may have often wondered why the butler had forgotten him. But had the butler recalled him immediately, Joseph might have been released, but would never have become God's man in Egypt to save his family during the famine. Slow was fast.

●*David* on two occasions could have taken the life of King Saul who was seeking to slay him. But David would not take the matter into his own hand, nor speed up the day of justice. Rather he said, "The Lord shall smite him; or his day shall come to die; or he shall descend into battle, and perish" (1 Sam. 26:10). The years as an exile provided David invaluable training for the years ahead, such as in waging war and in handling men.

●*Mordecai* reported a plot to assassinate King Ahasuerus, sparing the royal life, but received no recognition. Then one sleepless night the king learned from a reading of the records that Mordecai had saved his life and had never been rewarded. The outcome was a chain of events which led to wicked Haman's hanging, the elevation of Mordecai to premiership, and the monumental rescue of his people, celebrated to this day by the Feast of Purim.

Delays may mean later blessing. Dr. F.B. Meyer said, "There may have been long delays in the fulfillment of promises; but delays are not denials, and it is better to let the fruit ripen before you pick it." Someone referred to the "Delayed Blessings Office" in the Lord's treasure house, where the Lord keeps certain items till the right time to send.

A teenager was refused entrance to a college because he was under admission age, forcing him to wait a year. When a senior, he spotted the girl, a freshman, who ultimately became his wife. Had his entrance not been postponed a year, he would likely never have met her.

When Dr. Bob Cook, recently retired president of The King's College, was holding services for Youth for Christ in India, his group arrived at the airport for their plane home. It was in the early days of international travel. The airline clerk said, "I have no record of your reservations." In spite of pleadings, the clerk was firm. They had to wait two days before getting a flight. Later they learned that the earlier plane had gone down with no survivors.

Several metropolitan New York policemen, members of the "God Squad," were holding services in Pennsylvania one Saturday night. Leaving after the meeting, they made a wrong turn and ended up going in the wrong direction on the Pennsylvania Turnpike for a while. Because they had an early Sunday morning service, they began to speed a little. Suddenly they spotted radar. Sure enough, a Pennsylvania State trooper with lights flashing pulled them over. The trooper began to exclaim, "I don't believe it! I don't believe it!" The policemen thought he was shocked because they were policemen speeding. Then the trooper explained his amazement. "A few months ago my wife became reborn. She tells me about a group of reborn cops called the 'God Squad.' I've been sitting by the side of the road wondering how I could get in touch with the 'God Squad' when my radar catches a speeder. And the van says 'God Squad.'" They talked in the trooper's car. He received Christ. The policemen knew why they had been delayed by a wrong turn.

●*Delay is an excellent test.* Time is an excellent test. For the young lady who wonders if her admiration for her boyfriend is love or just infatuation, the best advice is—wait. Infatuation will die out; the real thing will grow.

Our projected plans should be subjected to the test of time to see if they are genuinely the will of God, or mere wishful thinking. The burden of divine leading will intensify; a mere subjective impression will fade. The saintly George Muller said, "Never be in a hurry in deciding questions of great importance, for whenever God speaks to us about anything, He always gives us time to recognize His voice."

●*Going slowly gives renewal.* A Christian worker who rarely took a day off was pressured by his family to take one day a week completely away from Christian duties. He soon realized that he accomplished far more in six days when he had a change of pace on the seventh.

Busy Christian workers sometimes point out, "Satan never takes a vacation." Since when do we make Satan our example? Rather we should look to Jesus Christ who one day said to His busy disciples, "Come ye yourselves apart into a desert place, and rest a while; for there were many coming and going, and they had no leisure so much as to eat" (Mark 6:31). Charles Spurgeon commented, "It's either come apart and rest a while, or you'll come apart."

An explorer who tried to force a bunch of nationals to make a fast march through the jungle found that, though incredible speed was registered for two days, on the third morning the nationals wouldn't budge, sitting and looking solemn. The chief explained, "They are waiting for their souls to catch up with their bodies."

Asked why he didn't wish to travel faster, an old Vermont farmer replied, "Because I figure I pass up more than I catch up with."

When Leonardo da Vinci was doing his famous painting *The Last Supper,* observers were critical of the long periods he would just sit in the cloister and meditate. His reply: "When I pause the longest, I make the most telling strokes." The psalmist said, "I wait for the Lord. . . . My soul waiteth for the Lord more than watchmen wait for the morning" (130:5-6). Taking time to be holy by reading the Word and prayer in the morning makes the day go better. Accomplishing things in the power of the Spirit requires waiting for God and not rushing ahead of Him. Waiting on the Lord is simply part of walking in the Spirit.

The late Dr. Peter Marshall, chaplain of the U.S. Senate, told of a Japanese father and son who farmed a little piece of land together, and several times a year sold their produce in a market in a city some miles away. The father was easy-going. The son was a go-getter.

As they loaded the ox cart one morning, the son calculated that they should reach the market by next morning. The father replied, "Take it easy. You'll last longer." The son argued, "By getting there earlier, we'll get better prices."

At noon they came to a little house by the road. "Your uncle lives here. Let's say hello."

"We've lost an hour already," complained the young go-getter. The son squirmed while the older men chatted an hour. Later at a fork in the road, the father chose the longer route. "It's more scenic."

"Don't you care about time?" the son retorted.

"Very much," said the father; "that's why I like to use it for looking at worthwhile things."

The son didn't look at the beautiful sunset, for he was busy counting the produce in the cart. He muttered, "Never again will I come with him. He's more interested in scenery than money."

Early next morning the son shook his father awake. At sunrise they came upon a farmer whose wagon had fallen into the ditch. The father insisted on helping. When the son objected, the father commented, "Someday you may be in the ditch." The son fumed over the loss of time.

By the time they resumed the journey it was almost 8 o'clock. Suddenly a great flash split the sky. Then a noise like thunder followed. The old man remarked, "Looks like a big storm in the city."

"If we hadn't loitered," gloated the son, "we would've sold our stuff and been on our way home by now."

"Take it easy," repeated the father. "You'll live longer."

Not till early afternoon did they reach the top of the hill overlooking the market town. What they saw made them speechless. Finally the son spoke, "Father, I see now what you mean."

They turned their cart around and drove away from what had been the city of Hiroshima (Catherine Marshall, *A Man Called Peter*, McGraw-Hill, pp. 317-319, quoted from a Billy Rose column, "Pitching Horseshoes," The Bell Syndicate).

God may slow you down, or stop you still, or place you on hold, or even put you in reverse, but He will get you where He wants you in His time. Divine on-timemanship means "slow is fast."

FOUR
CELESTIAL BANKING

To keep is to lose.
To give is to have

You probably remember the fable about the dog, carrying a bone, who saw his own reflection in water. He thought it was another dog with a bone and attacked the reflection to get the other dog's bone. In doing so, he dropped his bone into the water. Losing both bones, the greedy dog ended up with none.

Earthly thinking reasons, "Get all you can, and can all you get." This results in the ultimate loss of what you accumulate. On the other hand, divine logic says, "Share with others, and you'll be enriched." Proverbs puts it, "One man gives freely, yet grows all the richer; another withholds what he should give, and only suffers want. A liberal man will be enriched, and one who waters will himself be watered. The people curse him who holds back grain, but a blessing is on the head of him who sells it. . . . He who trusts in his riches will wither, but the righteous will flourish like a green leaf" (11:24-26, 28, RSV).

The more we keep for ourselves, the less we'll have in the end. The more we give to the Lord and others, the more we'll ultimately own. A man with a thousand dollars spends it on pleasure and has nothing to show for it. Another man spends his thousand buying hundreds of copies of the Bible, distributes them, and later learns that many have found forgiveness through the written Word. Someone said, "Christianity is a personal religion—*purse and all.*"

Jesus warned against laying up treasure on earth (by keeping it) because thieves, moths, and rust can make it disappear. Rather, He advised, lay up for yourselves treasure in heaven (by using it for the Lord's work) where nothing can destroy it (Matt. 6:19-20).

TO KEEP IS TO LOSE

Cash bonuses and glittering merchandise at times lure savings and loan customers to invest in relatively short-term certificates of deposit, though the total interest returns plus the bonus or premium may be lower than the amount competitive banks pay on the basis of interest on long-term deposits. Why do people accept a lower total yield? The answer, psychologists say, is the bias of human nature in favor of early, rather than long-term rewards. People like to have bonuses in their hands now, rather than even a larger amount of cash later. To grasp may be to forfeit. Why do people grab all they can?

It's human nature to acquire. In a college course on *Great Books,* the professor asked a coed which book she would choose if she could have only one. Quickly, she answered, "A checkbook!"

Man's fallen nature does not tend toward altruism but rather toward grabbing and grasping, having and hoarding. Man will do most anything to hold on to his money, or retrieve it. A man out for a walk found his path blocked by a wall. He remarked to his friend, "The wall is too high for me to climb." The friend seized the man's wallet from his pocket and tossed it over the wall. In a flash the man scrambled up over the wall and recaptured his wallet.

A rich man showed an acquaintance over his vast estate,

proudly pointing out all his valuable works of art and widely accumulated treasures. He expected to hear his friend's congratulations, but instead heard the warning, "Ah, these are the things that make death terrible!" A man and his money are not easily parted.

The reason we are so touchy about money is that we are so closely identified with our dollars. Money represents us: our toil, our time, and our talent. Money is concentrated personality, denatured manhood. Someone said, "The most sensitive nerve in the human body is the one that leads to the pocketbook."

We covet easily. "How much money do you want?" a millionaire was asked. His answer, "Just a little more."

We not only wish to keep what we have, but we want to add to it. Money charms. Enamored of his first million, a man heads for his second million. Solomon wrote, "He that loveth silver shall not be satisfied with silver, nor he that loveth abundance with increase" (Ecc. 5:10). The two words translated "covetousness" in the New Testament are literally "to have more" and "love of silver." Too often love of silver displaces love of God. Perhaps the most common form of idolatry is money worship. Paul plainly calls covetousness "idolatry" (Col. 3:5). The Decalogue, which begins by commanding love of the Sovereign, ends by condemning love of silver.

A little girl was asked, "What is money?" She responded without hesitation, "Why, it's to buy things with!" She hit the nail on the head. Money is a medium of exchange. Money represents purchasing power. Money is a means to acquisition. The rich man is called a man of means. He has the "wherewithal." But the urge to have more and more should be curbed. President Coolidge said, "Prosperity is an instrument to be used, not a deity to be worshiped."

The acquisitive-covetous nature makes it difficult for a person to be generous in his giving to church and charity. A denominational leader held a scheduled meeting in a village church to present the theme of biblical giving. Most of his audience earned a comfortable living. The speaker talked tithing, using charts and diagrams to show how the principle of each giving a tenth, if adopted, would easily double the financial income of their church. They seemed unenthusiastic. "There's a catch in it," responded one parishioner.

"I thought it was plain," said the speaker.

"Oh, it's plain enough," said the parishioner, whose shrewd eyes half closed as he continued, "but there's a catch in it all the same. I can see, if we adopt the plan, we'll be paying out more than we intend to give."

Grasping soon shrivels the soul. The acquisitive-covetous-hoarding spirit loses out sooner or later. Jesus said, "It is more blessed to give than to receive" (Acts 20:35). The joy of acquisition is momentary and minute compared to the delights of sharing. Satisfaction comes more from outflow than from income.

On the other hand, selfishness shrivels the soul. Miserliness makes for misery, both individually and collectively. Many years ago a church in Pennsylvania had a disagreement over giving to missions. The pastor and certain members took a stand against preaching the Gospel to the heathen. But others favored the inclusion of foreign missions in the budget. The division became so serious that the nonmissionary-minded members locked the others outside the meeting house. The pastor declared that he would remain at the church and preach as long as he had one person in the congregation. And that's what he did—for the congregation dwindled to one person. And then that man died. The church building, falling into a dilapidated condition, was sold and converted into a saloon. When the story appeared in print, all that remained as a memorial to those who threw their vote against missions was a cemetery where the church once stood. But those locked out because of their missionary giving zeal had to erect a much larger building where they continued their support for missionaries.

Improper acquisition is injurious. Judas grasped at 30 pieces of silver, but soon cast them at the feet of the chief priests and elders, then went out and hanged himself (Matt. 27:3-5).

Gehazi, Elisha's servant, pursued Naaman, whom Elisha healed, to ask for the money and garments his master had refused. Elisha, on Gehazi's return rewarded his greed with a rebuke and pronounced him afflicted with Naaman's leprosy (2 Kings 5:15-27).

Ananias and Sapphira found that hanging on to part of the sale price of their property while pretending to give it all was fatal (Acts 5:1-11).

Wealth gained hastily or wrongfully, such as by oppressing the poor, will dwindle and reduce to want. "Wealth hastily gotten will dwindle, but he who gathers little by little will increase it" (Prov. 13:11, RSV; also see 22:16, 22-23). A Greek proverb says, "No righteous man e'er grew rich suddenly." A Spanish saying reads, "Who would be rich in a year gets hanged in half a year." An Italian line puts it, "The river does not become swollen with clear water."

Money can cause family breakdown. Someone said, "Troubles in marriage often begin when a man becomes so busy earning his salt that he forgets his sugar." Neglecting his family, and disinterested in their activities, he finds himself alienated and isolated.

Knowing a man had plenty has led many a woman to set her feather in his direction. Gold diggers have broken up many a marriage or led men into ridiculous alliances.

Desire for more money has caused bad feelings between brothers and sisters. A man called out to Jesus one day, "Master, speak to my brother, that he divide the inheritance with me" (Luke 12:13). Jesus' answer was a warning against covetousness. Someone said, "Where there's a will, there's a relative or a lawsuit." Someone may gain a bundle but lose a brother.

Money and respect may be lost through thievery or disaster.

Papers repeatedly tell stories of jewel and fur robberies of homes of the wealthy. When you're rich, you become a potential target not only for thievery, but for blackmail, embezzlement, and kidnapping.

Banks have been known to fail. When Czechoslovakia fell into the Russian orbit a few decades back, the puppet government confiscated large sums of the people's money simply by claiming all the savings accounts in all the banks.

Many climb the ladder of success only to topple, losing the fortune that gave them a life of luxury. For example, Charles M. Schwab, first president of U.S. Steel, lived on borrowed money the last five years of his life and died in 1939 broke. Albert B. Fall, Secretary of the Interior under President Harding, accepted a bribe for leasing government-owned oil reserves to private companies and was sent to prison in 1931 and eventually pardoned to die at home. Wealth and reputation can vanish overnight.

Death strips us of everything. Even if we could successfully maneuver the ship of our finances around the shoals of thievery, bank failure, and financial disaster, death will ultimately relieve us of our possessions. We bring nothing into the world, and we take nothing out.

One word answers the perennial question, "How much did he leave?" The answer—everything. There are no pockets in a shroud. When Alexander the Great died, his hands were left outside the coffin: he had conquered the world, but he carried nothing with him into the hereafter.

When a preacher invited a middle-aged couple to church, they virtually slammed the door in his face. "We've set as our goal the accumulation of investments which will enable us to build a spacious new home and then to retire comfortably. Both of us work hard during the week, then spend weekends working on our new house. After we've saved all we need, we'll consider church."

A few years passed. The couple prospered. Their savings reached a substantial figure. Their mansionlike home was nearly complete. The week before they were to resign their positions and move into their new home, the husband, just 50, dropped dead of a heart attack.

The day he died the rich young ruler of the Gospels gave up all the wealth he wouldn't give up to follow Jesus.

Not only do we leave our money, but we lose control of it as well. Heirs decide how to spend it. A sign in a travel agency read, "If you don't go first class, your heirs will." A young man sporting a new $4,000 ring explained, "My father in his will left me $4,000 to buy a stone for him, and here it is!" The writer of Ecclesiastes realized that his heirs could squander his assets: "I hated all my labor . . . because I should leave it unto the man that shall be after me. And who knoweth whether he shall be a wise man or a fool? Yet shall he have rule over all my labor" (2:18-19).

The stingy have no treasure above. Those who hold on to their money on earth make no deposit of treasure in heaven. A rich man confined to bed with an incurable illness enjoyed the company of his little girl who spent hours in his room, often visibly puzzled why her big, strong daddy was lying there so helplessly. One day his business partners paid him a visit. The daughter somehow sensed an air of finality about the call. After they left, she asked, "Daddy, are you going away?"

"Yes, and I'm afraid I won't come back."

Then she asked, "Have you got a nice house there?"

The father, silent for a moment, turned convulsively toward the wall, muttering, "What a fool I've been! I've built a mansion here. I've made thousands of dollars, but I shall be a pauper there!"

A man may leave upward of a million without taking any of it upward.

TO GIVE IS TO HAVE
God has a way of rewarding us when we share with others. A little girl wore the necklace of plastic beads, given her by

her father, everywhere she went—to school, to play, to bed, even when she took a bath. She never took them off. How she loved those beads! But one day her father took her aside and asked her to give the pop-beads back to him. She stared at him in unbelief. Tears dimmed her eyes. He asked her again. She hesitated, for this was her dearest possession. Finally, crying, she took the beads and placed them in his hand. When she did that, he reached into his pocket, pulled out a string of real pearls, and placed them around her neck. To give is to get.

The last chapter of *Poor Little Rich Boy*, (The story of Colonel Robert R. McCormick) is titled "To Preserve a Treasure, Give It Away." According to his will, much of this millionaire's money was given to charitable institutions. Also his estate was opened to the public, and his fine house became a museum on a 500-acre green oasis west of Chicago.

Giving lays up a treasure in heaven. A man gave several thousand dollars to help build a church. Then he lost all he had in an economic crash. Someone said, "Had you kept that money you gave to start the church, you would have had enough to set yourself up in business again." He replied, "I would have lost that too. As it is, it's now in the bank of heaven yielding interest which will accumulate till eternity. Hundreds have come to know Christ through the church it helped build!"

John Bunyan wrote,

> A man there was,
> Some called him mad,
> The more he gave away,
> The more he had.

An old gravestone said,
> What I spent, I had;
> What I saved, I lost;
> What I gave, I have.

Someone said that the miser has misery in both worlds: he starves in this and is condemned in the next.

A little boy, holding his partly filled piggy bank, said to his pal, "To be sure my money is safe, I'm going to fill the rest of the piggy bank with water and put it in the freezer." Sometimes we freeze assets which should be thawed and circulated in places of need. Non-Christians recognize the need of putting money to use in a secular context. Dolly Levi, the heroine of Thornton Wilder's *The Matchmaker*, said, "I don't like the thought of it lying in great piles, useless, motionless, in the bank. Money should circulate like rain water . . . setting up a little business here, and furnishing a good time there." How much more should we Christians, after providing for our families and preparing for a rainy day through investments, be generous in giving to the Lord's work down here. As bountiful sowing in the field means bountiful reaping of crops, so generous giving here yields abundant dividends hereafter. Financial support of Bible-teaching churches, Christian schools, and other evangelical organizations lays up treasure above.

Another way of storing up eternal wealth is to give to the poor. To the rich young ruler, Jesus said, "Give to the poor, and thou shalt have treasure in heaven" (Mark 10:21). Augustine said that after giving our tithe we could place money "in the heavenly treasure by way of alms to the poor." A children's relief ad read, "You won't go broke giving 52 cents a day; you'll be richer." Incidentally, a person who deposits money in the bank of heaven must first open an account there by receiving Jesus Christ as Saviour.

It's not what we grab but what we give that makes us rich. As Jim Elliot wrote in his diary before his martyrdom by the Auca Indians, "He is no fool who gives up what he cannot keep to gain what he cannot lose."

Suppose we were told that ten years hence nuclear war would invalidate our present currency, making coins and bills no longer negotiable. Suppose pencils would be the acceptable currency. Property, stocks, bonds, money would all be worthless. Preachers would warn, "Money will be worthless. Seek pencils. Lay up pencils against the day of tragedy." While many would laugh and still go on saving money, the thoughtful person would reason, "Why go on accumulating what will be worthless in ten years. I'll turn every dollar into pencils." Similarly, money will be worthless in the world to come unless it has been transmuted into spiritual purposes. Jesus said, "Give alms; provide yourselves bags which wax not old, a treasure in the heavens that faileth not" (Luke 12:33).

Giving brings blessings now. Though giving lays up treasure for future heavenly bliss, the act of unselfish sharing brings immediate joy. A sense of satisfaction accompanies a genuine act of sharing. A poor man worked hard to buy an expensive gift for his mother. Asked how he could afford it, he replied, "It was worth it all to see my mother smile." John Greenleaf Whittier wrote,

> The joy that you give to others
> Is the joy that comes back to you.

The Israelite was told to open his hand to any poor in his midst, "because that for this thing the Lord thy God shall bless thee in all thy works" (Deut. 15:7-10). Similar blessing was promised those who left some sheaves at harvest time for the poor and the stranger (24:19-21). Proverbs says, "He that hath a bountiful eye shall be blessed" (22:9). Honoring the Lord with the firstfruits of their substance and bringing the tithe into God's storehouse would open heaven's windows of blessings to His ancient people (Prov. 3:9-10; Mal. 3:10). Jesus put it, "Give, and it shall be given unto you; good measure, pressed down, and shaken together, and running over. . . . For with the same measure that ye mete withal it shall be measured to you again" (Luke 6:38).

Billy Graham's mother was quoted by *Decision* as saying,

"The happiest, most joyful and most useful Christians are those who are giving in substance and service, generously proportionate to their receiving. In giving—blessings flow out, but joy flows in." When you spill perfume on others, you can't help spilling some on yourself.

A legend tells of a man who lived on the main highway through a busy town. One day an angel visited him with this message, "Someday the King of the Celestial City will call you to come and live with Him." The man thought, "I must have the finest suit to wear when I enter that city. And I must save my gold so that I shall have money when I arrive there."

One snowy night a stranger in ragged clothes knocked at his door. Through chattering teeth, he said, "The King of the Celestial City has asked me to visit Him and I'm on my way, but I don't have any good suit to wear. Besides, I'm shivering. I wonder if you could spare some clothes to keep me warm and help me look nice when I see the King." The man thought of his smart new suit but shook his head no, for thought he, "What would I wear when I myself go to see the King?"

The next night came another knock. This time a poor woman stood there. "Please, sir," she said, sobbing, "I'm a widow. My husband died last year, leaving me with an only girl. She's so sick that only an operation can save her life, but I have no money for the doctor or hospital. Could you loan me some gold? I'll work hard to repay every ounce. Please help me!" The man thought of his gold but turned the weeping woman away thinking, "What money would I have to buy things in the Celestial City if I gave her my gold?"

One day word came that the King of the Celestial City wanted to see him. So he ran upstairs to don his new suit, but when he opened his closet, he found that moths had eaten gaping holes in both coat and trousers. When he looked for his gold, it had turned to brass. He had to make the trip to see the King in his moth-eaten suit and without any gold. The next day he saw his neighbor approaching the Celestial City. He was likewise wearing an old suit and was penniless. But when he neared the gate, the King ran to meet him. The minute the King touched the neighbor, his worn suit was miraculously transformed into a handsome new suit and his pocket was immediately filled with gold pieces. When the man looked astonished at what was happening to his neighbor, the King explained, "That night you turned away the shivering beggar and did not give him your suit, he went next door to your neighbor and he gave him his finest suit. The next night when you refused to give any gold to the poor widow to save her sick daughter's life, your neighbor gave her the little gold he owned. You kept your treasure down there, but he sent his on ahead!"

Faithful giving to the Lord's cause is one reason some believers will have an abundant entrance into the everlasting kingdom. We should never sacrifice the eternal on the altar of the temporal. The wise man said, "Cast thy bread upon the waters, for thou shalt find it after many days" (Ecc. 11:1).

The Holy Land has two good-sized seas. The Sea of Galilee, alive, sparkling, and lovely, is used today by fishermen as it was in the days of Jesus. The other, the Dead Sea, is polluted and saturated with chemicals so that nothing lives in its waters. Why is one fresh, and the other stagnant? Because the Dead Sea gives nothing out. No river flows from it, though the Jordan River flows into it. In contrast, the Sea of Galilee not only has the Jordan flowing into it, but also flowing out. The Sea of Galilee is alive because it gives.

To keep is to die. To give is to gain.

Helen Steiner Rice wrote:

> The more you give, the more you get;
> The more you laugh, the less you fret
> The more you do UNSELFISHLY.

The more you live ABUNDANTLY.
The more of everything you share,
The more you'll always have to spare.
The more you love, the more you'll find
That life is good and friends are kind.
For only WHAT WE GIVE AWAY
ENRICHES US FROM DAY TO DAY.

FIVE
ABUNDANT LIVING

To find your life is to lose it.
To lose your life is to find it.

young Christian asked his uncle, "Why was I born?" His uncle replied, "If you will be obedient, God will let you know."

Walking down the street a few minutes later, the youth came across a burning theater. Braving the flames, he brought out one person after another until he had saved 13. Knocked unconscious by a piece of falling timber, he was taken to the hospital. Opening his eyes for a brief moment just before passing into the presence of his Lord, he whispered to his uncle, "Now I know why I was born. That I might save those 13."

A few months later a wild-eyed man approached the uncle on the street. Talking excitedly, he kept saying, "I was in a burning building some time ago and I saved myself. I saved myself!" Just then a man came along and led him away, explaining, "This man was in a theater that burned some months ago. He left his friends and saved himself, and the thought of it has driven him mad."

The road to abundant living is through doing the will of God. Jesus put it, "He that findeth his life shall lose it; and he that loseth his life for My sake shall find it" (Matt. 10:39). Jesus uttered this principle because of coming persecution in which heathen judges would try to persuade believers to renounce their faith. "Save your life; don't throw it away." Jesus warned that by recanting they might save their physical life, but would lose eternal life. Yet if faithful to Him, though losing their physical life, they would gain eternal life.

The paradox contains a deeper meaning. If our main goal in life is to selfishly gain popularity, possessions, and position, we'll miss the higher values of life, and suffer dissatisfaction. But if we set our affection on Christ and things above, we'll discover the abundant life. We lose by finding. We live by dying.

Charles R. Weede in his poem "The Conquerors" contrasts two men who both died at 33. One conquered the known world; the other was a seeming failure. Alexander the Great died at Babylon after leading vast armies, shedding much blood of his foes, and enslaving millions of people, all for self. Jesus died at Calvary on a cross, had no armies, and shed His own blood. One lived to blast; the other died to bless. Alexander is dead, but Jesus rose to life forevermore, King of kings, and today His followers number in the millions.

David Livingstone, nationally decorated pioneer explorer, opened up the interior of Africa for missionary work, at the same time fighting the debasing slave traffic wherever possible. At a great memorial service in London for Livingstone, a gray-haired old man could only wail and weep while others were rejoicing. He explained, "David and I were boys together. He gave his life to Christ and His service, but I chose to go my own way. Now he is honored by the whole nation. And look at me! My life has been a tragedy."

When Livingstone's body was deposited in Westminster Abbey, Mr. Punch, England's journalistic jester, without any thought of humor remarked, "Let marble crumble; this is Livingstone." Essayist Emerson wrote, "The mass of men worry themselves into a nameless grave while here and there a great unselfish soul forges himself into immortality." Livingstone buried himself for Jesus' sake in Africa. Today he is remembered on many continents.

TO FIND YOUR LIFE IS TO LOSE IT

Trying to find life through selfish pursuits does not satisfy. We may buy many things, but they leave an empty feeling. Our finest possessions—jewelry, furniture, finery—all tarnish, wear out, or fade, and often are carried away by the junkman or antique dealer. The pearl seeker who drowns at the moment of clutching his gem is a supreme loser.

Pleasure does not satisfy permanently. Despite a search to find contentment in amusements, America has the highest per capita boredom of any spot on earth. Power and fame are fleeting. Napoleon, exiled to an island, died a lonely death. Hannibal took poison. Caesar was assassinated. Mussolini was executed. Hitler blew himself to bits in a bunker. Marilyn Monroe, excelling in beauty, money, and fame as a movie actress, took her own life.

Possessions do not give satisfaction. Tolstoy tells of a man who started out at dawn with the promise that he could have for his own every piece of land he could encircle from sunrise to sunset. As the day wore on, the lure of the rich soil stirred him to a faster pace. As the sun was setting in the west, he slipped off shirt and shoes, and with heart beating like a trip-hammer forced himself to the utmost. Just as the sun fell beyond the horizon, he flung himself forward, fingertips touching the goal, and dropped there—dead. Taking a shovel, men gave him his land, a strip of soil six by two.

Fame does not satisfy. The men of Babel wanted to make a name for themselves, so they built a tower to reach up to God. Who can name just one of those builders? Their names perished with the tower.

Then there was Lot. When the countryside became too small for their increasing flocks, Abraham and Lot decided to separate. Graciously, Abraham gave Lot his choice of fields. Lot selfishly chose the well-watered plains of Jordan, where he could expand his livestock and grow rich. Also, the nearby city would give opportunity for business advancement, political appointment, and social elevation. Perhaps his daughters could marry well, avoiding entanglement with any of Abraham's smelly, rustic farmhands. So he pitched his tent toward Sodom, a city of iniquity from which the sin of sodomy derives its name. Lot thought his choice would bring him "life."

But he discovered that gain was loss. First, he was captured by warring kings and might have died a slave had not Uncle Abraham rescued him.

As he gradually moved toward the suburbs of Sodom, then into the city, where he became an official, his associations tended more to the wicked folk of Sodom, and less with Abraham, the friend of God. Lot's spiritual life dulled, though his income may have skyrocketed. Someone imagined his business signs all round the metropolis like, "Lot's lots for sale," or "You get a lot when you buy a lot from Lot." With fewer than ten righteous in the city, the Lord "delivered just Lot, vexed with the filthy conversation of the wicked" (2 Peter 2:7).

His family life suffered. His sons-in-law laughed at his warning. His wife became a pillar of salt. How significant that Luke 17:32, which says, "Remember Lot's wife," is followed by, "Whosoever shall seek to save his life shall lose it; and whosoever shall lose his life shall preserve it" (v. 33).

Lot lost a lifetime of service. With home broken, possessions cremated, and himself saved as by fire, all his works proved to be wood, hay, and stubble. Our last glimpse finds him in a mountain cave, tricked into a drunken stupor by his daughters, who, carrying the morals of Sodom with them, committed incest with their father, begetting two nations, Moab and Ammon, both of which continually harassed Israel.

Lot sought life and lost it. But Abraham, dying to his own selfish choice, heard the Lord say after Lot separated, "Lift up now thine eyes, and look from the place where thou art northward, and southward, and eastward, and westward; for all the land which thou seest, to thee will I give it, and to thy seed forever. And I will make thy seed as the dust of the earth" (Gen. 13:14-16; also see chapters 18 and 19).

A Canadian preacher told of a wealthy family who, claiming their daughters could not meet eligible, high-society young men in his church, moved their membership into a large, liberal church. Their eldest daughter later married a reputedly important man from a so-called fine Southern family, whom she met at a fashionable resort hotel in northern Ontario. The parents were delighted at the union. Not long after, the father died one Saturday playing golf at his country club, leaving his wife a rich woman. A few months afterward, someone broke into her mansion, chloroformed her temporarily, blew open the safe, and stole thousands of dollars, jewelry, and bonds. Authorities later revealed that the man who administered the chloroform was none other than the young man who had married the victim's daughter, the woman's own son-in-law!

Self-centeredness leads to loneliness. In his book *The Man Who Loved Islands,* English writer D.H. Lawrence tells of a man who, enjoying to be by himself, sought solitude. With his savings, he bought an island. But finding no happiness, he sold the island and bought another, then another and another. He spent years moving from island to island, till finally he became insane. If we get wrapped up in ourselves and our interests, and withdraw from the needs and friendship of others, we'll find ourselves hopelessly alone.

Samuel Beckett's nihilistic philosophy is vividly portrayed in his play *Breath.* Only 35 seconds in length, without human actors, the only prop a pile of rubbish on the stage lit by a light that brightens moderately then fades to dimness, the play has no words. It begins with a recorded cry of an inhaled breath followed by an exhaled breath, then the identical cry at the end. Those who live for self will find life a meaningless, short breath.

A missionary translator at Inter-Varsity's Urbana 1984 Conference said, "The worst thing that could ever happen to a person is to live life through never having a cause worth dying for."

TO LOSE YOUR LIFE IS TO FIND IT

If we aim at earth, we get little or nothing. If we aim at heaven, we get earth thrown in too, for we find the abundant life here. John warned not to love "the world, neither the things that are in the world." The reason is that "the world passeth away, and the lust thereof; but he that doeth the will of God abideth forever" (see 1 John 2:15-17). Those who turn from self-centeredness to do God's will are the real winners. Such losers are finders.

A Scottish pastor asserted that he knew of sanitariums in both England and Scotland that had to close because of lack of patients soon after World War II broke out. Opportunities to help others, such as in air raids, cured them. He cited a woman in the third basement of a church which served as an air-raid shelter and Red Cross depot. "Notice that woman yonder wearing the uniform of a volunteer nurse. Two years ago she was an invalid, and a problem to herself and everyone else. You ought to see her now when the siren sounds. Instantly, she's on the job, often working all night long caring for the injured and dying. Everyone loves her" (John Sutherland Bonnell, *No Escape from Life*, Harper, p. 205). Immersing herself in a cause, she found "life," no longer a victim of worry and fear. Waldo Emerson said, "No man can sincerely try to help another without helping himself."

True on the natural plane, this principle operates also on a higher level. Jesus spoke of losing one's life "for My sake." It's when we lose ourselves in Jesus' cause, in the work of His kingdom, that we find real life (Matt. 10:39). Losing our life for the highest purpose results in the abundant life.

What happened to two bean seeds. A Gospel tract tells the parable of two bean seeds which had been sold with others to the local hardware store. Self-willed told Surrendered that he was planning an escape, so no one would ever purchase him and put him in the cold ground, as had happened to other seeds. One day, about to be dropped into a bag for a customer, he jumped off the side of the scoop onto the floor, and rolled under a nearby radio. Here Self-willed enjoyed the bright lights illuminating the area around him, heard the popular music coming from the radio, and felt himself a part of the wonderful world with all its attractions. He forgot all about Surrendered, who by this time had been taken to the garden of a buyer and completely covered over with soil. All went well till one day the store owner decided to sweep the floor. Self-willed was suddenly dashed into a blazing furnace and quickly consumed.

Weeks later Surrendered emerged from the ground a lovely green plant with leaf after leaf, then blossoms, then finally long, green pods with many seeds therein. Surrendered soon forgot how he had been dropped into the earth and trampled on, now that he was living and could do his share in helping others.

Many like Self-willed seek life in the world's glamour but find it empty. Those like Surrendered who die to self find themselves alive and bringing forth fruit in God's garden.

This parable, of course, was based on Jesus' words, "Except a corn of wheat fall into the ground and die, it abideth alone; but if it die, it bringeth forth much fruit" (John 12:24). Then follows our upside-down factor, "He that loveth his life shall lose it; and he that hateth his life in this world shall keep it unto life eternal. If any man serve Me . . . him will my Father honor" (vv. 25-26).

It may well be that Jesus spoke about corn falling into the ground and dying because He had just been tempted not to die. Greeks had just approached Him as admirers of His masterful teaching ability, perhaps hinting that he should continue in that profession. But Jesus resisted the temptation, knowing that if He did not go to the cross, no one would be saved. Rather he said, "I, if I be lifted up from the earth, will draw all men unto Me" (v. 32).

Jesus is the supreme example of living through dying. Because He died, millions have eternal life today. Also, though He never wrote a book or started a school, more books have been written, and more schools founded, because of Him. Also, every letter we date, every official document, every newspaper, every calendar—all refer indirectly to Him, for time is reckoned from His birth, either B.C. (before Christ) or A.D. *(annō Dominī*—in the year of our Lord). The very instrument of His death, the shameful cross reserved for foreigners, slaves, and criminals, has been transformed into an instrument of triumph. Imagine wearing a miniature electric chair, or gallows, or gas chamber as a decoration. Yet millions today the world over wear crosses on their lapels as badges of honor.

Real fame from God's viewpoint. Men may have their names inscribed on marble monuments for feats of fame. Someday these monuments will fall in fragments. Those honored in God's book are the names that stand over graves where self was buried long before the body died, like the five young men martyred by the Auca Indians deep in the Ecuadorian jungle.

Jesus asked Peter, Andrew, James, and John to leave all for Him. Dying to their boats, nets, and families, they became fishers of men whose names have been immortalized wherever the Gospel has gone. Matthew surrendered a lucrative tax-collecting occupation to follow Jesus. His name has been honored through the centuries as the author of the first book of the New Testament.

Would the lad with the loaves and fishes keep his little lunch for himself and satisfy his hunger urge? By giving his meal to Jesus, he became the instrument whereby the Lord fed the 5,000.

Moses could have lived on at the Egyptian palace, adopted son of Pharaoh's daughter, member of the royal family, enjoying the pleasures and treasures of a great land. But in saving his life, he would have lost it, to be buried an unknown mummy in some forgotten Egyptian grave. But choosing to die to ambition, fun, honor, and wealth, Moses is honored worldwide today.

Was Billy Sunday a baseball player or an evangelist? He was an outstanding baseball player in his day, but most recall him as a foot-stomping, arm-waving, chair-smashing evangelist. Yes, we remember him to a degree for the impact he made on the baseball world, but much more for the impression he made on human lives. His daring, speedy base-running could bring the crowd to its feet, but we remember him more for the quarter-million people he brought to their feet and down the sawdust trail to make decisions for Christ. We forget his exploits on the diamond. We recall the jewels he will have in heaven.

We find life by denying self. TV commercials recommend self-indulgence. *Try this./Taste that./Wear this./Drink that./You only go round once in life, so grab all the gusto you can get!* But the Apostle Paul wrote that we ought "not to please ourselves. . . . For even Christ pleased not Himself" (Rom. 15:1, 3). He also wrote about being crucified with Christ and letting Christ live through us (Gal. 2:20). He also wrote of carrying in our bodies the death of Jesus so that the life of Jesus might be manifest in our bodies (2 Cor. 4:10). Jesus Himself equated losing one's life with self-denial (Matt. 16:24-25).

Athletes practice self-denial. At summer camp a college boy deliberately resisted overeating. He watched teenagers gulp down huge quantities of fried chicken, gravy, chocolate sundaes, and hot rolls dripping with butter, while he ate very simply. Though a normal youth who enjoyed food, he had to weigh 20 pounds less by the end of the summer to qualify for the sport he loved. Paul urges Christians to keep their bodies disciplined in order to be winners (1 Cor. 9:24-27).

We must even die to family if it interferes with following and serving Christ. Jesus warned, "He that loveth father or mother more than Me is not worthy of Me; and he that loveth son or daughter more than Me is not worthy of Me" (Matt. 10:37). Two verses later He spoke of finding and losing life, illustrating the importance of placing Him ahead of all earthly relationships.

When God asked Abraham to sacrifice his only son Isaac in whom everything important to Abraham was concentrated, he did not flinch but was in the very act of complying when suddenly God intervened. Abraham received Isaac back as from the dead. The promise of a multitudinous progeny was fulfilled.

Vividly, I recall a scene at a railroad station in Hamilton, Ontario, Canada. A crowd from my church had gathered to bid farewell to a middle-aged man heading back to the Orient for another missionary term. His parents, over 80 years of age, and not professing Christians, stood on the train steps just before departure gulping their sorrow, shedding profuse tears between sobs. A hundred people sang, "God be with you till we meet again." The missionary realized the possibility (which became a reality later) that he would never see his parents on earth again. But this did not deter him. God used him mightily that term in the Orient.

Sometimes a potential marriage partner has to be surrendered. Jean determined to answer God's missionary call and went off to nurses' training. Away from home and Christian friends, she became engaged to a young resident doctor, though he showed minimal spiritual interest. The wedding date was set, but Jean had a spiritual battle on her hands. Did her love for John outweigh her love for

God? In desperation she turned to the Bible and read, "If any man will come after Me, let him deny himself, and take up his cross, and follow Me" (Luke 9:23). It was settled. She broke the engagement. Years later on the mission field she confessed that, though the decision was heartbreaking at first, all regret passed as she discovered that supreme happiness that comes from doing God's will. For her and all who make a similar decision Jesus promised, "There is no man that hath left house, or parents, or brethren, or wife, or children, for the kingdom of God's sake, who shall not receive manifold more in this present time, and in the world to come life everlasting" (Luke 18:29-30).

Losing one's life often involves loss of creature *comforts*. Paul wrote to the Philippians that at that time only Timothy had enough concern for them for him to inconvenience himself on their behalf (Phil. 2:20-21). Not a person was sufficiently self-disinterested to make the trip to Philippi. All others were too involved in their own affairs to volunteer for the job. Timothy doubtless found deep inner reward in self-forgetting labors for the Lord.

When a couple was asked to pick up a new pupil for Sunday School, they refused because it would mean leaving a little earlier and driving four blocks out of their way. Their refusal sounds radically and ridiculously different from the heroes of faith listed in Hebrews 11 who were tortured, scourged, jailed, stoned, sawn in two, killed by the sword, or destitute from persecution. This world was not worthy of them, but they will receive a rich heavenly recompense.

Art Beals in *Beyond Hunger* tells of Coleen who worked morning, afternoon, and evening in a refugee camp on a small, rocky island off the coast of Malaysia. She was teacher, mother, counselor, and friend to several hundred minors, ages 2 to 15, who had survived dangerous voyages from the shores of Vietnam. In the evenings she worked patiently with those struggling to learn English. The camp seemed never to sleep. All day long, announcements blared over the loudspeaker. Dirt, frustration, and insomnia were constant. Asked how she could live in this bedlam day after day, Coleen replied with a weary smile, "I wouldn't trade my work here for any experience in my life. I'm having the time of my life!" (Multnomah, p. 196-97).

A missionary and two strangers walking over the mountains of Tibet discovered a beggar dying of cold and begging for help. The strangers argued that if they stopped to help the beggar, they would freeze to death, so went on their way. But the missionary lifted the beggar and carried him. The warmth of the beggar's body kept the missionary warm. A little later he came across the frozen corpses of the two strangers. Losing his life, the missionary found it.

St. Francis of Assisi wrote:

> Lord, grant I may seek rather
>   to comfort than to be comforted;
>   to understand than to be understood;
>   to love than to be loved;
> for it is by forgetting self
>   that one finds
> it is by forgiving
>   that one is forgiven,
> it is by dying
>   that one awakens to eternal life.

A chapter in Charles Colson's book *Loving God* titled "Life and Death" contrasts the zest of a 91-year-old resident of an old people's home in Columbus, Georgia with dozens of others waiting for their meaningless existence to end. When Colson received a letter from Grandma Howell telling how she was corresponding with prison inmates and how she was handling their problems, he determined to visit her when Prison Fellowship held a rally in her city.

He found her in an old soot-covered brick downtown high-rise building. The atmosphere was depressing—no pleasant banter, no youthful voices, but instead rows of wheelchairs lined in front of a blaring TV, bodies hunched on overstuffed sofas and worn upholstery, dozing or gazing spacily.

Knocking on Myrtle's door, Colson heard a firm "Come in" sounding so unlike a woman about to die. She excused herself for not getting up, pointing to a walker by her chair. Her modest-sized room had one window, a bed, a 12-inch TV set, a dresser, a mirror, the two chairs they sat in, and a fragile desk crowded with Bibles, commentaries, and piled-high correspondence. Though living in pain, she began, "Writing to inmates has filled my last days with joy." She told how, depressed with the death of her husband, loss of her home, declining health of her oldest son, and then the death of her youngest ("baby boy"), she felt the call of God to write to prisoners. She wrote a letter addressed simply, "Atlanta Penitentiary, Atlanta, Georgia." Inside she told of her love for those in a place where they had not planned to be, and if they wanted to hear from her, she would answer every letter they wrote. The letter was passed on to the prison chaplain. Eight inmates wrote her.

Since then Myrtle Howell has corresponded with hundreds of prisoners all over America. She prays for God's help with every letter she writes. She said she didn't do much of anything but write to inmates, read, and study the Bible, watch a few Christian TV programs, and be pushed in her wheelchair to and from the common dining hall for her meals. She repeated, "I've had the greatest time of my life since I've been writing to prisoners."

On the way out Colson was again overwhelmed by the sad scene. Sunken eyes of other residents reflected depression, despair, emptiness, and anger at loved ones who had deserted them and at cruel fate that had left them helpless, just sitting and waiting for their meaningless existence to be swallowed up in darkness.

Meanwhile upstairs, Myrtle with her 91-year-old grin was probably back at her desk writing to prisoners, alive with joy and purpose. She had long since learned heaven's upside-down paradox that by giving up her life she had gained His life.

The question often comes, "Why on earth are we here?" Someone answered wisely, "For heaven's sake." When we lay on the altar whatever we cherish most—reputation, project, position, title on our office door, plans for our self-generated destiny, and lose ourselves in Christ's program—we find abundant life.

On finding something, people often recite, "Finders, keepers; losers, weepers." Jesus reversed this sing-song saying to make it, "Finders, weepers; losers for My sake, keepers."

SIX
HEAVENLY ARITHMETIC

Much is little.
Little is much.

*S*teven L. Rogers, detective on the Nutley (N.J.) Police Force and founder of God Squad, a metropolitan New York area ministry to police officers, in his book *Cops and God* (Logos, pp. 68-104) tells of an assignment soon after he joined the force in 1977. The mayor asked him, along with another officer, to look into the problem of young people running rampant in parks and residential areas, drinking alcohol, taking drugs, and vandalizing property. When numerous complaints centered on mobs of teenagers terrorizing residents living near a railroad trestle, the two officers decided to make this their number-one priority.

After two weeks' surveillance, they realized they were not dealing with just a few kids having fun, but with throngs of young people, some of whom were drug addicts with minds out of control. Learning that Friday was always the big party night, and that the drug-supplier was an 18-year-old named Bruce, whom all dubbed "Mr. Big," they reported a plan of action to the Detective Bureau. Since they estimated as many as 50 would gather for the party, they requested a minimum of five men to assist in a raid the next Friday night. The two detectives felt it would be "suicide" to attempt the raid by themselves, but their request for more men was turned down.

Steve and his partner wondered how they could ever apprehend that many people. They also pondered why these youths seemed to evaporate into thin air and escape arrest. Both born-again Christians, the officers asked God's help. Soon after, they discovered a well-worn path camouflaged by leaves and brush. The path led through bushes and shrubbery to a hillside; here they found a cave, the inside of which looked like a one-room apartment. This clubhouse, right under a railroad trestle, was furnished with two old armchairs, a double-bed mattress, pillows and blankets, and a large woven rug. Using their flashlights, the officers found a cache of pills, beer, whiskey, and bags containing traces of marijuana, plus stacks of pornographic magazines. The detectives now knew the youths had eluded the police by hiding in the cave until the puzzled cops left.

Steve and his partner planned to raid the teenagers' cave the following Friday night. Dressed in jeans and sports shirts and carrying empty beer bottles to blend into the crowd, they climbed the embankment by the railroad tracks. Screams, shouts, and curses filled the night air. They counted 30 youths and picked out Bruce, the ringleader. They wanted to apprehend him first but realized how badly they were outnumbered. *These kids are in a reckless state of mind,* they thought, *potential killers, almost out of control, like a group of rioting prisoners.* The detectives prayed for guidance as to when to make their move.

At 1 A.M., three hours after first arriving, Steve and his partner began walking toward the group, eyes fastened on Bruce. A girl spotted them and screamed. Deciding to apprehend her first, the detectives tore down the embankment after her, through a row of houses into the street, where they arrested her, and called for a marked car to pick her up. Returning to the tracks, they headed in after

Bruce, wondering how many had remained in the hide-out. *They probably feel like trapped animals and will attack us if we go in*, they thought. *But they have no idea we know the existence of their hiding place, so we'll have the element of surprise on our side.*

Quoting a verse about God giving His "angels charge over thee to keep thee in all thy ways," they crept cautiously toward the entrance to the cave. Steve felt a chill rush up his spine, and he broke out into a cold sweat.

Praying, with courage rising, standing straight and tall, they entered the cave. "Freeze!" shouted Steve. Not a person moved or spoke. His partner walked over to Bruce and asked for the bag of pills in his hand. Steve read them their rights and arrested 12 for violating the narcotic laws of New Jersey. One by one the detectives marched them out of the cave, radioing police headquarters for a van to take them to the station. Steve turned to Bruce. "Why didn't you try to attack us when we entered the cave?"

"You think I'm crazy or something? There were at least 20 of you guys, and it would have been stupid to think about attacking or running," he replied.

"Twenty? No, Bruce, there were only 2 of us and 12 of you."

"Wait a minute," he said, scratching his head. Turning to his girlfriend, he asked, "How many cops came into the cave?"

"I don't know for sure," she responded, "but at least 25!"

"Those weren't cops you saw," Steve replied; "those were angels!"

Without God the dozen delinquents were really few. But just two policemen, with God, were many. Here's another divine paradox in the upside-down kingdom: without God more is less; with God less is more.

Consider the unseen army at Dothan. Steve Rogers' story reminds us of an Old Testament incident. When the king of Syria wanted to capture Elisha who was visiting Dothan, he sent horses, chariots, and a great host by night to surround the city. Early next morning as he saw this vast army encompassing Dothan, Elisha's servant lamented, "Alas, my master! What shall we do?" Elisha replied with a prayer, "Lord, open his eyes that he may see." The servant then saw the mountains full of horses and chariots of fire round about Elisha. When the enemy came to apprehend Elisha, the Lord blinded them, permitting Elisha to lead the helpless Syrians ten miles away (2 Kings 6:13-23). The great host of Syrians were no match for Elisha supported by the invisible army of God's angels.

When Dr. Clyde Taylor, who for many years was associated with the National Association of Evangelicals, was a young missionary in the jungles of Peru, he played Gospel recordings for the chief of a tribe and explained why he had come to the area. Later at dusk, Taylor spotted a big canoe and realized it would take several men to row it. Hearing whistling, which he knew meant signals, and sensing something wrong, Taylor and his friends decided to stay out in the jungle that night. Nothing happened. Two years later that chief became a believer. Shamefully, he admitted, "We intended to kill you that night. But you were too many. On your roof were crowds of men, all in white robes." Taylor believes that God used angels to protect him.

MUCH IS LITTLE

In God's arithmetic there are times when more may be less. The biggest army without God stands powerless before a tiny band backed up by God.

An army of 135,000 was routed by a band of 300. When the Midianites, Amalekites, and the children of the east marshaled their armies against Israel, they numbered 135,000, according to Judges 8:10. Gideon's forces totaled only 32,000 (7:3). Outnumbering the Israelites four times, the Midianites seemed destined for an easy victory over Gideon. But to show He does not play the numbers game, God had Gideon excuse from battle all who were in any way fainthearted. The Lord said to Gideon, "The people that are with thee are too many for Me to give the Midianites into their hands, lest Israel vaunt themselves against Me, saying, 'Mine own hand hath saved me'" (7:2). Gideon must have done a double take when he saw 22,000 walk away to return home, leaving just 10,000 to fight 135,000.

But divine reasoning considered 10,000 still too large a number. So the Lord devised a test to eliminate some more. Almost all of them, 9,700, drank by putting their mouths right into the river. But 300 lapped like dogs, lifting their hands to their mouths as they alertly kept watch. These men became Gideon's army.

If this small group, reduced from 32,000 to 300, could rout an army of 135,000, certainly no one could credit numbers. Using a trumpet, torch and pitcher at a prearranged signal in the middle watch of the night, the 300 surprised their enemy, who half-awake and confused, fought against their own soldiers, killing 120,000 and then the remainder in a later mopping-up operation. The many Midianites were really few; the 300 few with God's help were many.

David's mistake in counting numbers. When in late life David called for a census, it was an exercise in pride. Learning that his men fit for fighting totaled 800,000, how easily enamored of numbers he might have become, tempted to pick on weaker nations, and thus undermine his own country internally. Perhaps he wanted to boast that his armed forces equaled those of his enemies, forgetting victory belongs to the Lord. He should have known that "no king is saved by the size of his army" (Ps. 33:16, NIV).

Record-keeping is permissible, but we must exercise caution when we emphasize the size of our membership, the 2,000 Sunday morning attendance, and our $200,000 given to missions last year.

The majority is not always right. Senate Chaplain Richard C. Halverson in his *Perspective* (Concern Ministries, Inc.) says, "If a thing is right, 10,000 saying it does not make it more right. And if a thing is wrong, 10,000 saying it is right will not make it so! A good leader does not count opinion . . . he weighs it! A trustworthy elected official is not the one who capitulates to numbers."

The ten spies were wrong in their advice against advancing into the Promised Land, whereas the minority report of Caleb and Joshua to attack was right (Josh. 13–14). Because almost everyone in a college class believes premarital sex is right does not make it right.

LITTLE IS MUCH

Americans live and breathe statistics. Success is often measured in terms of numbers. How tall is the building? How many thousand books were sold? How huge is the plant? Is his income in six figures? We boast of the biggest newspaper circulation, the oldest inn, the fastest car. Many are happiest when they have more of something than their neighbors.

But the truly wise person views qualitatively, not quantitatively. The Lord isn't so interested in how many people attend a church, but what kind of people. Granted, godly and zealous people should win more to their church, so that quality leads to quantity. Yet mere quantity is not the criterion of spiritual success. The widow's two mites counted more with the Lord than the combined total of all the rich men's contributions.

When a person gives his tithe to the kingdom, the Lord can make the remaining nine-tenths go farther than ten-tenths. When a person devotes one day a week to rest and worship, the Lord can make the six remaining days more productive than the full seven spent on self. In other words, nine-tenths of our income with God total more than ten-tenths without Him. And six days with God are more than seven days without Him.

A newly married young couple faithfully attended Sunday School, Sunday morning and evening worship, and midweek prayer and Bible study. Both worked. They needed time evenings to paint and fix their newly rented apartment. Yet both taught Sunday School. She played in the orchestra, and both sang in a young adult ensemble. Asked how they could devote so much time to the Lord's house, the husband replied, "We believe in tithing our time. It'll go farther. We'll get more done."

Only a few find life. Toward the end of the Sermon on the Mount Jesus warned, "Enter by the narrow gate, for the gate is wide and the way is easy that leads to destruction, and those who enter by it are many. For the gate is narrow and the way is hard that leads to life, and those who find it are few" (Matt. 7:13-14, RSV). Significantly, the main streets of many towns and cities, the streets lined with places that allure away from God, are called *Broadway.* Because the majority walks the broad way does not make it the right way. It's the few who find life.

When God sent the Flood, only eight entered the ark and survived. The majority rejected Noah's warning.

When Abraham interceded with God to spare Sodom, the Lord agreed to do so if 50 righteous could be found. The Lord lowered the number to 45, then 40, 30, 20, and finally 10. But 10 could not be found. Ten righteous (quality) folk would have spared the lives of a large quantity of unrighteous.

Rahab, a heathen harlot, seemed a most unlikely candidate for rescue from the city of Jericho. But she showed her trust in the living God by hiding the spies, putting a scarlet cord in her window, and bringing her family under the same protection. Made quality by faith, she married an Israelite, became an ancestor of Christ, and appears by name in the genealogy of Christ (Matt. 1:5). Except for her family, all the rest of the Jericho inhabitants perished.

The parable of the lone, lost sheep found by the Master

out in the wilderness taught that there's more joy in heaven over one sinner who repents than over 99 just persons who need no repentance (Luke 15:7).

We cannot judge the truth of Christianity by the number of its adherents. Muslims easily outnumber Christians in our world, but that doesn't make the Muslims right.

A new pastor visited a couple on the membership list who never came to church. Five years previously the church had a goal of 50 new members by Easter Sunday, but reached only 48 by the Saturday before. A zealous deacon had gone to the home of this couple, urging them to join. Over their objection that they had never attended the church, the deacons persuaded them to let their names be recommended for membership. They told the new pastor, "We joined, but we've never been back since." Those who are hurried into church membership without experiencing the new birth add only quantity, not quality.

A godly few can win battles against great odds. The Lord promised His ancient people that five would chase a hundred, and a hundred would put 10,000 to flight (Lev. 26:8).

Had the Israelites listened to the 2 "full faith" spies instead of to the fearful 10, they would have not wandered 40 years in the wilderness.

One with God is a majority. The Lord promised the Israelites, "When thou goest out to battle against thine enemies, and seest horses, and chariots, and a people more than thou, be not afraid of them. . . . For the Lord your God is He that goeth with you, to fight for you against your enemies, to save you" (Deut. 20:1, 4).

In the final stage of conquering Canaan, Joshua was opposed by several kings who gathered their forces, "much people, even as the sand that is upon the seashore in multitude, with horses and chariots very many. . . . The Lord said unto Joshua, 'Be not afraid because of them, for tomorrow about this time will I deliver them up all slain before Israel' " (Josh. 11:4, 6). God kept His word.

David knew who gave him victory over his enemies time and time again. He sang, "The Lord is my light and my salvation; whom shall I fear? . . . Though an host should encamp against me, my heart shall not fear" (Ps. 27:1, 3). Safety did not reside in numbers but in the omnipotent God.

Lone Elijah put to rout 450 prophets of Baal. Later as Elijah lamented that he and only he was left of all the prophets of God, the Lord told him that 7,000 others had not bowed the knee to Baal (1 Kings 19:14-18). The prophet should have known that whether 1 or 7,000, quality could defeat quantity, especially after his victory at Mt. Carmel.

Elijah's reputation of superhuman power was well known even in the palace. This is why King Ahaziah sent 50 soldiers to inquire of the prophet if he would recover from his serious illness. The king felt so large a military group would challenge Elijah to show whether Ahaziah or the God Elijah represented was the stronger. Fire from heaven consumed the 50 soldiers. The king sent another 50 who were likewise consumed. The third band of 50 begged for their lives. This time Elijah went with the soldiers to the palace and told the king that he would not recover (2 Kings 1:9-18).

Time and time again an army of fewer numbers defeated forces of superior size. Abijah's 400,000 routed Jeroboam's 800,000 "because they relied upon the Lord God of their fathers" (2 Chron. 13:3, 18).

An Ethiopian army of a million men attacked King Asa whose army numbered several hundred thousand fewer. Asa cried unto the Lord, "In Thy name we go against this multitude" (2 Chron. 14:11). The Lord smote the Ethiopians.

When King Jehoshaphat was told of a "great multitude" of Moabites and Ammonites arrayed against him for battle, the king prayed, "O our God, wilt Thou not judge them? For we have no might against this great company that cometh against us." The Lord answered, "Be not afraid nor dismayed by reason of this great multitude, for the battle is not yours, but God's" (20:1-2, 12, 15).

When Sennacherib lay siege to Jerusalem, he terrified its inhabitants by pointing out their military deficiencies and boasting of his sure victory. But King Hezekiah encouraged the people of Jerusalem, "Be strong and courageous; be not afraid nor dismayed for the king of Assyria, nor for all the multitude that is with him, for there be more with us than with him. With him is the arm of flesh, but with us is the Lord our God to help us and to fight our battles" (32:7-8). Soon after, the Lord slew 185,000 Assyrians, forcing Sennacherib to return humiliated to his own land, where not long after his own sons executed him.

In the 17th century Samuel Rutherford, a godly Covenanter who suffered for the Gospel, wrote Lady Kenmure who was also going through persecution: "Worthy and dear lady, in the strength of Christ, fight and overcome. You are now alone, but you may have for the seeking, three always in your company, the Father, the Son and Holy Spirit" (*Spiritual Disciplines,* edited by Sherwood Wirt, Crossway Books, p. 114).

A few sold out to God can accomplish far more than a multitude of halfhearted. Those with quality spiritual lives will pack a much greater wallop than large numbers of nominal believers. The mixed multitude that came out of Egypt with the Israelites caused trouble later (Ex. 12:38; Num. 11:4-6).

Daniel and his three friends who resisted Nebuchadnezzar's dietary orders turned out to have healthier appearances. Remember the song that challenges, "Dare to be a Daniel; dare to stand alone"?

Our Lord's invitations during His ministry never aimed for high numbers of respondents, but rather seemed to have a cautioning effect. "Follow Me, but first count the cost," He said in effect. "Don't put your hand to the plow and then look back. I'd rather have a fewer number of higher quality." Jesus warned against quantity of harvest lacking reality. The seed that suddenly bears fruit may sprout from shallow soil. Or fruit that gets choked may spring from a heart filled with the deceitfulness of riches or the cares of this life.

From the standpoint of enlisting devoted disciples, the Lord Jesus seemed a failure. At the end of His ministry He had only 12 close associates, who repeatedly displayed imperfections, weaknesses, and failures. But the Lord had worked patiently to develop quality. Their exceptional training, anointed by the Holy Spirit at Pentecost, changed this nondescript, ragtag, dullish, slow-to-learn gang of throne-climbers and deserters into a united, godly band of courageous evangelists. Within three months after Christ's ascension, their number had increased to thousands. Within three years, their scattering converts had carried the Gospel to surrounding countries. And within three decades their influence had spread through much of the Roman Empire with converts even in Nero's palace.

A church, stationary and stagnant for decades, suddenly came to life, resulting in numerous converts, increased attendance, generous missionary giving. It was later learned that three or four women had been meeting faithfully for years on Saturday nights to pray. "If two of you shall agree on earth as touching anything that they shall ask, it shall be done for them of My Father" (Matt. 18:19).

A few started the Christian Business Men's Committee meetings. A few started Youth for Christ. A few started Child Evangelism. John Wesley said, "Give me a hundred men who love God with all their hearts, and fear nothing but sin, and I will move the world."

What one can do. Even when the few shrinks to one, much can be accomplished. Napoleon was called Cent Mille by his men, because his presence on the battlefield was worth 100,000 men.

A woman said to her husband, "All I know about politics

is that my vote usually cancels out yours." But one vote can have a wide effect. Thomas Jefferson was elected President by just one vote of the electoral college. So was John Quincy Adams. One vote kept Aaron Burr from becoming President of the U.S. One vote saved President Andrew Johnson from impeachment. One vote elected Oliver Cromwell to the famous Long Parliament and sent Charles I to the gallows.

Joseph was able to save his father and brothers from starvation in famine, and to provide them with a possession in the "best of the land" of Egypt. Esther's plea to her husband, King Ahasuerus, saved her people from extermination. Though only one, these single individuals had come to their kingdoms for just such occasions.

A little captive maid in the home of the leprous Syrian commander-in-chief, Naaman, was bold enough to recommend the Prophet Elisha who became instrumental in his healing.

Much credit for the Reformation goes to one man, Martin Luther. The emphasis on biblical exegesis that extends to the evangelical pulpit today is credited to one man, John Calvin. Scottish reformer John Knox, who always stood his ground fearlessly against formidable opposition, said, "A man with God is always a majority." One man, William Carey, a cobbler, burdened for the salvation of the heathen, studied and prayed at his bench, and against opposition which included clergymen formed a missionary society, went to India as a missionary, and today is known as the father of modern missions.

A group of railroad conductors on an excursion arrived late Saturday night in a Southern city. They were discussing a trip proposed for the next day. Sunday morning, when about to start, one of their number was missing. They found him wearing his best suit. "Aren't you going with us?" they asked. He replied, "No, I'm going to church. That's my habit every Sunday." When the conductor started for church, 150 others joined him.

In his book *Beyond Hunger,* Art Beals under the caption "Little is much when God is in it!" tells the story of Dulal Borpujari, born into a privileged Brahmin family in India. He was transformed by the Gospel and exchanged the ease and security of his social position for a life of risk and deprivation. Mechanically gifted, he invented a plow that revolutionized farming in India. Simple, inexpensive, and able to lift some of the heavy toil from the backs of peasant farmers, this plow is in wide use all over India to this day. Losing his business, he established himself in Calcutta; here he was moved with the dire poverty of that city and concerned by the lack of opportunity for its young men. Dulal established a vocational training school which also provided work through the manufacture of beds, wheelchairs, and other hospital equipment. Larry Ward, founder of Food for the Hungry, needing a third-world national with technical skills, tapped Dulal to manage the affairs of this rapidly growing relief agency in Asia and to serve as an international vice-president. Says Art Beal, "Dulal is just one example of many third-world nationals who have either risen out of poverty or cast aside privilege in order to make an important difference" (Multnomah, p. 77-78).

As we attempt to carry the Gospel to our world, we should remind ourselves of Christ's promise, "Lo, I am with you alway." One of Anne Kiemel Anderson's favorite challenges is "You and Jesus can change the world."

It's incredible what one plus God can do!

SEVEN
GENUINE JOY

Happy but miserable.
Miserable but joyful.

A wealthy king reportedly confessed, "I have reigned half a century in peace, honored by my subjects, feared by my enemies, respected by my allies. Riches, pleasure, and power have been at my beck and call. No earthly delight has escaped my experience. In this most fortunate and felicitous situation, I have carefully counted the days of genuine happiness which I have enjoyed. They total 14!" To all outward appearances he possessed every right to be happy. Yet he was unhappy.

A godly member of my church entered a New York City hospital for treatment of his serious physical condition. The doctor, noting his patient's cool attitude and bright cheerfulness, cautioned, "Your optimism is inappropriate for your situation." The patient responded by stating the biblical reason for his hope. This same patient, after two years of satisfactory health during which he maintained his employment, again entered a New York City hospital, this time for tests on his heart. A different doctor asked, "How can you be so calm?" Pausing, the patient replied, "Doctor, you asked for it," and proceeded to give his testimony of faith in Christ. To all appearances this patient had much cause to be unhappy. Yet he perennially possessed a joyful outlook.

Unbelievers are often miserable in the midst of their so-called joys, whereas believers are often joyful in the midst of their miseries. Emperor Nero grumbled on a throne, while the Apostle Paul sang in a dungeon.

HAPPY BUT MISERABLE

Laughter does not necessarily mean joy. Too often the loudest laugh hides the hollowest heart. "Even in laughter the heart is sorrowful; and the end of that mirth is heaviness" (Prov. 14:13). Many depressed individuals possess a smiling depression, so called because they smile to cover up inner sadness. Their philosophy is, "Eat, drink, and try to be merry, for tomorrow we die."

Many act happy who underneath are unhappy. Those round, jovial faces that stare at us from postcards, stationery, bumper stickers, and posters often feature the word *Smile.* They imply that we can place a smile on our face as easily as we stick a stamp on a letter or put a glove on our hand. But a good actor can look happy even when his heart is sad.

A despondent man asked a doctor for a cure for his blues, so the story goes. The doctor suggested an amusing book. "I've tried that and it hasn't worked," replied the patient who was a stranger to the physician. The doctor made some other suggestions, all of which the patient had tried. Finally the doctor said, "I've only one more idea, and if this doesn't work, I don't know what will. That new circus in town has a clown who keeps the audience in stitches of laughter. If he can't drive away your blues, I don't know who can."

Replied the man, "alas, I am that clown."

A magazine article on comedian Jackie Gleason carried the subtitle "Tragic Facts, Never Before Told, of the Torment behind the Comedy Genius Who Earned Three Million Dollars a Year. He is lonely, tormented, fearful" (from the book, *The Lonely Millionaire* by Jim Bishop).

Many opt for death. About every 30 minutes someone in the U.S. commits suicide, likely after seeking in vain for happiness. Worldwide, half a million suicides are reported annually. *The New York Times* estimated that in a recent year in the U.S. about 5 million people of all ages—children to oldsters—had tried to kill themselves. Suicide is the second leading cause of death among college students.

A young woman who won all the honors as a high-school senior, an outstanding musician, lead actress in all the school plays, popular with students and faculty, confessed to a pastor's wife, "I would go home and cry. I was not happy."

Many middle-aged people also exist without joy. Realizing they will never reach their goals, or on the other hand, having attained seeming success, these joyless individuals find inner satisfaction eluding them. One couple wrote a syndicated columnist, "We have a well-furnished home, a new car, and money in the bank. Our two sons have finished college and are happily married and doing well. We have excellent jobs and our combined income makes it possible for us to live comfortably. So why are we writing this letter? Because suddenly we find life empty and boring. Are we different, or does this happen to all couples in later midlife?"

It's not surprising that elderly people account for one quarter of reported suicides, happiness having vanished. Dr. Vernon Grounds says, "Joy is about as rare as the bald eagle." Samuel Johnson once remarked that the human race is a vast assemblage of individuals who are counterfeiting happiness.

Happiness is elusive. Remember the paradox that says if you seek happiness, it will elude you? And it goes on to emphasize that real happiness comes to you when you are simply doing your duty and not making happiness your goal.

But through the ages people have sought happiness only to fail to find it. It happened in the late 1690s in France during the reign of Louis XIV. By the 1690s the king's court "gayly fiddled . . . while France burned." Debauchery had reached its last, desperate stage with young ladies and gentlemen "dying of boredom, longing to enjoy themselves all the time, but never finding anything to satisfy their insatiable desire for pleasure," according to the book *At the Court of Versailles* by Gilette Ziegler (Dutton). Within they were saying, "Already all things start to fade: gardens are less bright, colors less vivid, meadows less green, waters less limpid. The shadow of death hovers over all things."

Countless youths today are in a similar situation. Already bored in early high school by the usual pleasures, they seek greater excitement in drugs, perversion, or violence. But the law of diminishing returns guarantees letdown. Since the second piece of cake is less satisfying than the first, and the third piece even less so, those who pursue a life of thrills eventually get big letdowns. Indeed, organizations for suicide report that peak periods for victims who die at their own hands follow holidays.

People seek happiness in the wrong places. People often reason, "If I had money, land, stocks, three cars, a swimming pool, a boat, and plane, then I'd be happy. The have-nots think that if they struck it rich they'd be satisfied; the haves know this isn't so.

Ernest Hemingway's suicide perplexed his biographer, who in his foreword listed what the famous writer had going for him: he had won both the Nobel and Pulitzer Prizes; he had a home in Idaho's Sawtooth Mountains; an apartment in New York; a specially rigged yacht to fish the Gulf Stream; apartments available at the Ritz in Paris and at the Gritti in Venice; a sturdy marriage; and friends everywhere. Yet this literary genius put a shotgun to his head and killed himself. The biographer, though Hemingway's close friend for 14 years, admitted he did not know why (*Papa Hemingway*, A.E. Hotchner, Random House).

Millionaire Jay Gould said, when dying, "I suppose I am the most miserable man on earth." Steel magnate Andrew Carnegie remarked, "Millionaires seldom smile and never laugh."

Pleasure doesn't last. Pleasure, when rationally controlled, has its proper place. Even sinful delights yield a degree of pleasure (Heb. 11:25). But such pleasure is short-lived, disappointing, and limited. Hedonism leads to the dead-end street of frustration, boredom, and burned-out ashes. Robert Burns wrote:

> Pleasures are as poppies spread;
> You seize the flower, the bloom is dead.

The libertine lives it up. Everyone thinks him happy. But is he? Often the morning after a night on the town his mouth has a rotten wood taste, his head feels as if it will explode, and his liver acts up. Yet next night he dives into another round of sensual gratification. Far from experiencing happiness, he's inwardly disgusted with himself.

Lord Chesterton said, "I have run the silly rounds of pleasure, and by no means desire to repeat the nauseous dose." The woman at the well, after affairs with at least six men, was still seeking the Water of Life (John 4:15).

Power isn't the answer. Many think conquest, position, and power can bring inward satisfaction. In his early career Mussolini exclaimed, "I am obsessed by one wild desire. It consumes my whole being. I want to make a mark on my era with my will." Then with great fierceness he scratched the back of a chair, muttering. Mussolini was later executed, a miserable man.

Svetlana Stalin said of her dictator-father, "I believe that the conqueror himself was not happy at all. On the contrary, there came complete loneliness, unhappiness, disappointment, and suspicion in all around him."

Sir Winston Churchill, according to the *New York Times,*

uttered as his last sentence, "I am bored with it all."

Fame fails you. Benjamin Disraeli (Earl of Beaconsfield), who enjoyed his share of fame as prime minister of England, wrote, "Youth is a mistake; manhood a struggle; old age, a regret."

Essayist Charles Lamb remarked, "I walk up and down thinking I am happy, and knowing I am not."

Some with names up in bright lights are dissatisfied within. In 1978 Chris Evert-Lloyd, then two-time Wimbledon women's tennis champion and winner of more than a million dollars the previous year, took four months off from professional tennis because, according to the Associated Press, "she realized she was not happy."

Some try drugs and drink. Many think a party dull without drinks. Though intoxicants temporarily stupefy and drown out troubles, true joy is not imbibed from a bottle. Consider the problems drugs have caused prominent athletes, evidently unhappy despite fame and wealth. Most shocking were the deaths this last year of basketball star Len Bias and pro football's Don Rogers within days of each other.

In his book on the ministry of Teen Challenge, Director Don Wilkerson reflected of the thousands of drug addicts who came to his ministry: "Not a single one has ever told us that he had found that deeper meaning through dope, or that drugs had given him the happiness, kicks, or thrills that he had sought. What's more, never have I heard of anyone anywhere who was happy that he had become addicted" (*The Gutter and the Ghetto* by Herman Weiskopf, Word, p. 168).

If ever a person was qualified to pass judgment on the ability of earthly goods, games, and glory to satisfy the human heart, it was King Solomon. He tried mirth, magnificent mansions, might, money, music, material possessions, and mistresses. He indulged in every pleasure, sparing nothing to try to fill the emptiness of his life (Ecc. 2:1-10). But his conclusion was "all is vanity" (2:11; 1:2).

Modern psychologists would call it *existential vacuum.*

America's prosperity has not brought true happiness. Never has a generation been bombarded by a more sophisticated network of media to eat more, play more, and buy more. Someone called the U.S.A. the rich fool of Jesus' parable, swollen to the size of a nation. With the highest per capita income in the world and its countless gadgets, U.S. citizens should be supremely happy. Instead, we consume massive quantities of tranquilizers.

An American was describing the glories of his country to an African leader. After a recital of America's industrial genius and material prosperity, the unimpressed African solemnly asked, "But are your people happy?"

There's no happiness unless we get to the root of the problem. Our nocturnal tranquility is often disturbed by such questions as, "Where did I come from? Why am I here? Where am I going? How may I get right with God?" Because the wee small hours give time to face reality, they have been called "night questions."

C.S. Lewis said that whatever we are longing for, whether it be the "Island" in *Pilgrim's Regress,* or the climbing of some mountain or the sailing of some sea, these things will never fully bring joy, because what we are really longing for is God. And God can be known only through Jesus Christ.

Man cannot live by bread alone, nor by money, fame, power, or pleasure. God designed salvation through Jesus Christ to satisfy the deepest longings of the human heart, and to give life abundant. As Augustine put it, "Man was made for God and will not rest until he rests in God." Till man finds that divine satisfaction, he will remain basically unhappy and unfulfilled, wistfully sighing for a long-missing note.

MISERABLE YET JOYFUL

Dr. Carl Lundquist, president of the Christian College Consortium, told how a visit to the Lutheran Sisters of

Mary in Darmstadt, Germany had a special impact on him. The order started as a result of World War II bombings on that city in which many people were killed. Several young women, thinking the worst, found to their delight, after much searching, that their friends were still alive. In gratitude to God, they declared the traditional vows of chastity, poverty, and obedience. *Christianity Today* (July 12, 1985) commented that one would expect to find a sense of gloom in the lives of people "without romantic fulfillment, without financial security, and without personal freedom." Yet the description of these Lutheran Sisters of Mary is that "they twinkle a lot." Though seemingly deprived, these ladies exude a deep sense of joy and celebration.

Joy differs from happiness. Happiness depends on satisfying happenings, whereas joy is independent of circumstances. Ocean gales, ripping across the Atlantic, can catapult waves 50 feet high. Yet 50 feet below, the water is perfectly calm. Similarly, happiness is like the surface of the sea, ever changing. Joy is like the ocean bed, ever the same.

To be happy all the time is impossible, for all of us will face unhappy circumstances to some degree. But joy can abide.

Bible people who rejoiced in suffering. Many of David's psalms suddenly break forth in praise in the midst of trouble.

The night before His crucifixion Jesus spoke of His own joy, which doubtless gave Him strength to sing a hymn in the face of His coming ordeal, and then to endure the terrible agony of the cross (John 15:11; Matt. 26:30).

The joy which shone on the face of Stephen as he made his defense before the Sanhedrin enabled this first martyr of Acts not only to stand the stoning, but also to pray for his tormentors (Acts 6:15; 7:59-60).

Peter and John could depart from the presence of the Sanhedrin after a cruel beating, rejoicing that they were counted worthy to suffer shame for Jesus (Acts 5:40-41).

Peter would later write that when fiery trials came believers were to rejoice (1 Peter 4:12-13).

In the Philippian dungeon, with their feet shackled and backs covered with coagulated blood from the vicious Roman whips, Paul and Silas sang praises at midnight. Later when Paul wrote to the Philippians, he had every right to command them to "rejoice always" (4:4). In fact, when he wrote them, he was again a prisoner, this time in Rome, and chained to a guard 24 hours a day. Facing the ordeal of a trial and possible execution, he was still rejoicing, practicing what he preached. He rightly characterized his attitude in suffering "as sorrowful, yet always rejoicing" (2 Cor. 6:10).

These believers rejoiced in trouble. The early Christians had the reputation of rejoicing in suffering. In A.D. 200 Cyprian, bishop of Carthage, wrote a friend a letter in which he described the wickedness going on in the Empire, including wars, robbery, piracy, arson, and men murdered in the amphitheater. He spoke of the "selfishness and cruelty and misery and despair under all roofs. It is a bad world . . . an incredibly bad world. But I have discovered in the midst of it, a quiet and holy people who have learned a great secret. They have found a joy which is a thousand times better than that of any of the pleasures of our sinful life. They are despised and persecuted, but they care not. They have overcome the world. These people . . . are Christians, and I am one of them" (G. Ernest Thomas, *What Jesus Was Like,* Pulpit Press, pp. 63-64).

A Good News Publishers tract titled "Seven Men Went Singing into Heaven" told of seven prisoners behind the Iron Curtain, at their request, facing the firing squad with faces uncovered. Then with hands raised to heaven, they heartily sang "Safe in the Arms of Jesus."

Is it possible to rejoice when death snatches a loved one, making us "long for the touch of a vanished hand, and the sound of a voice that is still"? Naturally, we grieve deeply.

Jesus wept. But natural sorrow can be attended by supernatural joy which empowers us to sorrow differently from those who have no hope. Like Paul, we can be sorrowful, yet rejoicing.

Not only in sorrow, but we can also be joyful in sickness and suffering. A new pastor was asked to visit a woman who had been an invalid for 16 years. She was nearly blind. Her arms and legs were twisted. She was never without pain. Yet she asked the pastor to join her in singing "There Is Sunshine in My Soul Today."

Fanny Crosby, blind from wrong medication put in her eyes when she was six, wrote the following at the age of eight:

> O what a happy soul am I!
> Although I cannot see.
> I am resolved that in this world
> Contented I will be;
> How many blessings I enjoy
> That other people don't!
> To weep and sigh because I'm blind
> I cannot, and I won't.

Before she died, in her 95th year, she had composed more than 4,000 hymns, including some which remain favorites today.

Sources of genuine inner joy. Billy Graham's mother wrote: "Upon what do we depend for our happiness? Is it bright sunshine and clear skies? No. Fine clothes and lovely homes? No. Is it money? Is it fun? No. Fun is a passing experience and does not always express joy. Joy, for the Christian, is the result of an inward sense of peace which comes from a right relationship with God. Our first joy is the consciousness that Christ is ours. Homes and houses don't create Christian happiness. Christ has to bring it" (Morrow Coffey Graham in *Decision*).

Jesus Christ came to earth to do a work that makes

possible the filling of that vacuum in human hearts. Because of His sacrifice on the cross, we may have our sins forgiven, strength for daily living, and the guarantee of future bliss.

Great joy comes through the realization of sins forgiven. The Psalmist David wrote, "Blessed is he whose transgression is forgiven, whose sin is covered. Blessed is the man unto whom the Lord imputeth not iniquity" (Psalm 32:1-2). The 3,000 who experienced the joy of forgiveness at Pentecost "did eat their meat with gladness" (Acts 2:46). When the people of Samaria heeded the Good News preached by Philip, "there was great joy in that city" (Acts 8:8). When the Philippian jailer and his family believed on the Lord Jesus, they rejoiced (Acts 16:34). Paul wrote, "We also joy in God through our Lord Jesus Christ, by whom we have now received the atonement" (Rom. 5:11).

The day after his conversion, Alan Redpath, who later became pastor of Chicago's Moody Church, read Romans 8:1, "There is therefore now no condemnation to them which are in Christ Jesus." Overjoyed at the thought of no judgment for his sins, he underlined the words *no condemnation* so heavily that he defaced a number of the following pages.

We exult not only on entering the state of blessedness, but we also "rejoice in hope of the glory of God" (Rom. 5:2). Glory refers to the ultimate future blessedness guaranteed to believers. Jesus told His disciples to rejoice because their names were written in heaven (Luke 10:20). Either death or Christ's return will dispatch us into His presence to be eternally with Him. Jesus said, "Let not your heart be troubled," then spoke of heavenly mansions He would prepare for saints (John 14:1-3).

Joy comes not only from forgiveness of the past and anticipation of a glorious future, but also from the provision of strength for the present with all its trials. Dr. James E. Means, associate professor of homiletics at Denver Conservative Baptist Seminary, who lost his wife through cancer, has written a poignant account of God's dealings in his life. In *Tearful Celebration* he writes:

> Consider Paul's words "sorrowful, yet always rejoicing" (2 Cor. 6:10). He was simply indicating that in the ugliness of profound grief the Christian is supernaturally enabled to rejoice. The hallelujahs of joy reverberate on broken heart strings. My sorrow touches every part of my life, yet I sorrow not as those who have no hope. My rejoicing is not that of happy feelings; it is triumph in trial and confidence in a supreme God. The true joy of the Lord is divine enablement, not effervescent emotions. The real taste of celestial joy is discovering that I can conquer sorrow through Him that loved me. . . . The place of grief becomes the sacred place of intimacy with the suffering Servant. It is sacred and joyous not because it is pleasant, but because we are sustained there by the secret consolations of a Master who never forsakes. That is our pure joy" (Multnomah, pp. 45-46).

It is in Christ that we have redemption through His blood, in Him that we have our inheritance, in Him that we are blessed with all spiritual blessings. Therefore, it is in Christ that we are to rejoice, not in spiritual gifts, nor in opportunities for service, nor in growth in grace. Joy belongs to the person who finds fulfillment in Christ. We cannot always rejoice in circumstances, but we can rejoice in our Lord.

Jesus' fullness of joy did not come from material things, for He was born poor and died poor. Nor from creature comforts, for He had nowhere to lay His head. Nor from human relationships, for He was rejected by His flesh-and-blood brothers, and forsaken by His followers. Nor from human praise, position, or power, for He was hounded by His enemies till they succeeded in executing

Him. His joy came from a right relationship with His Father. He said, "I do always those things that please Him" (John 8:29). Basically, His joy came as a result of obedience.

Joy has been called the ecstasy of eternity in a soul that has made peace with God and is ready to do His will. A right relationship with Christ involves both being and doing, both standing before Him and serving Him. "If you know these things, happy are you if you do them," said Jesus (John 13:17). A missionary doctor, asked if he was underpaid, replied, "Is there any greater remuneration than simple thanks of a mother for whom you have just delivered the first living child in 13 pregnancies? Or the gratitude of a blind man who left your hospital seeing the path for the first time in many years? Or the joyful radiance on the face of a man who just received Christ as his Saviour—a man who will die within a few months from an inoperable cancer?"

No, not happy is he who has made a fortune, who can write a check in six figures, who spends each winter in a tropical resort, who has his name up in bright lights, who has a mansion, who moves in high political circles. But joyful is he who possesses that fruit of the Spirit, a deep-down exultation that transcends common delights and overcomes suffering, sickness, and sorrow, always able to hum a calm gloria or shout an enthusiastic hallelujah.

EIGHT
BLESSED FREEDOM

Freedom leads to slavery.
Slavery leads to liberty.

*I*f you travel by ship between Lake Erie and Lake Ontario, you have two possible choices: the Niagara River or the Welland Canal. The Niagara River is the only natural connection between these two lakes. But its wild rapids and great falls (Niagara) render it useless as a waterway. The other choice, the Welland Ship Canal, opened in 1932, exceeded in cost then only by the Suez and Panama Canals. A marvelous feat of engineering, the Welland Canal is the largest lift-lock in the world, overcoming the 326½ feet difference in level between Lakes Erie and Ontario by the eight locks that punctuate its 28-mile length. When a ship moves into a lock, the gates—2 at each end with each set weighing 1,000 tons—shut. Then depending on which direction the boat is headed, the water level slowly drops or rises 46½ feet, taking 20 minutes.

The Niagara River, so much broader than the narrow Welland Canal, flows from a mile to 4 miles wide at places. But the narrow Welland Canal hems ships into a narrow passage 310 feet wide. If a ship could make the river route, it could travel the 33 miles in 3 hours, whereas traversing the Canal's 28 miles takes 8 hours, because of the delay passing through the 8 locks.

So which would you choose: the Niagara River, wide and fast, or the Welland Canal, narrow and slow? No one in his right mind would choose the wider Niagara River, for if not dashed to pieces by the rapids, you'd tumble over the falls to almost certain death. It's a choice between the broad way of the river that leads to destruction, or the narrow way of the canal which leads to the desired destination.

Toward the end of the Sermon on the Mount, Jesus warned, "Enter ye in at the strait gate, for wide is the gate, and broad is the way that leadeth to destruction, and many there be which go in thereat; because strait is the gate, and narrow is the way which leadeth unto life, and few there be that find it" (Matt. 7:13-14).

Here's another paradox of the upside-down kingdom: freedom brings servitude, and slavery brings liberty. The Lord challenged Israel with two choices: "Behold, I set before you this day a blessing and a curse; a blessing, if ye obey the commandments of the Lord your God . . . and a curse, if ye will not obey the commandments of the Lord your God" (Deut. 11:26-28). The license of throwing off restraint would mean the confinement of curses, such as a blighted harvest, poor health, defeat by enemies, scattering among the nations, and ultimate bondage by a foreign conqueror. But the narrowness of obedience would open into the broadness of blessings such as numerous progeny, abundant harvest, long life, and victory over enemies (Deut. 27–28). These choices were graphically portrayed by the use of two mountains. Priests standing on Mt. Gerizim pronounced blessings while priests on Mt. Ebal announced curses.

Many passages from Proverbs reinforce this paradoxical principle. Those who walk the narrow path of wisdom find the glorious liberty of honor, protection, prosperity, and long life. But those who walk the broad path of evil stumble in darkness and violence (4:10-14; 11:6). "He that tilleth his land [requiring limiting self-discipline] shall have plenty of bread [freedom of abundance], but he that followeth after vain persons [license] shall have poverty [restriction] enough" (28:19). "Whoso despiseth the Word [license] shall be destroyed, but he that feareth the commandment [narrowness of obedience] shall be rewarded (13:13).

Paul taught that a Christian, though a slave, is the Lord's free man. Also, a free man who is a believer is Christ's slave (1 Cor. 7:22). The irony often existed in a household where a Christian slave was really free in God's evaluation, while a non-Christian master was really a slave to his own sinful nature. People who do their own thing to the breaking of God's commands become slaves to sin, whereas those who become slaves to Christ discover the freedom to do righteousness (Rom. 6:16-18).

FREEDOM LEADS TO SLAVERY
Too much liberty yields a restrictive penalty. A man rocked a boat to see if it would tip. He drowned. A man dissipated through night hours to see if it would really injure his health. It led to an early grave. A youth stepped on a nail to see if it would go through his shoe. It did and also pierced his foot. We want the freedom to smoke, and we end up with emphysema and cancer. We take the liberty of overeating and find ourselves slowed down with obesity. We take the line of least resistance by never exercising, and wonder why we have poor cardiovascular circulation. "There is a way that seemeth right unto a man, but the end thereof are the ways of death" (Prov. 16:25).

What would happen if police went on strike, giving citizens the opportunity to do whatever they pleased. This occurred on October 7, 1969 in Montreal, Canada, one of the world's largest cities. Because of what resulted, the day has been called Black Tuesday. A burglar and a policeman were slain. Forty-nine persons were wounded or injured in rioting. Nine bank holdups were committed, almost a tenth of the total number of holdups the previous year, along with 17 robberies at gunpoint.

Usually disciplined, peaceful citizens joined the riffraff and went wild, smashing some 1,000 plate glass windows in a stretch of 21 business blocks in the heart of the city, hauling away stereo units, radios, TVs, and wearing apparel. While looters stripped windows of valuable merchandise, professional burglars entered stores by back doors and made off with truckloads of goods. A smartly dressed man scampered down a street with a fur coat over each arm. With no bothersome police around, anarchy took over. Had the strike continued longer than a day, people gripped by fear would have locked themselves in their cellars or fled the city.

A state of turmoil often existed in the days of the judges in Old Testament times. Incidents toward the close of the Book of Judges include the making of an idol, installing a family priest, kidnapping a priest, slaughter of the Danites, homosexual advances, abuse and murder of a concubine, and the slaying of thousands of Israelites in tribal war. The last verse of Judges sums up the reason for these sordid stories: "In those days there was no king in Israel: every man did that which was right in his own eyes" (21:25). Freedom led to anarchy.

Imagine a baseball game without rules! A batter could have ten strikes if he wished, and the first baseman could move the bag 100 yards away from home plate. The game would become bedlam. Picture a busy intersection without traffic lights. Untangling the tie-ups would take hours, especially if angry people took matters into their own hands. To violate God's rulebook of life or to disregard His moral traffic lights is to court disaster. License is bondage.

The freedom to wag the tongue leads to losing friends. The freedom to kick in any direction leads to getting kicked back. The freedom of driving on the wrong side of the road leads to collision and tragedy. The lawbreaker soon suffers the penalty of a jail cell, discovering that the way of the transgressor is hard (Prov. 13:15).

Rebellion against divine authority brought servitude. Our first parents, stepping beyond divinely prescribed boundaries in the Garden of Eden by eating the forbidden fruit, discovered the bondage of toil, exile from the garden, and the curse of death.

Pharaoh, who said, in effect, "No one, not even God, is going to tell me what to do," learned the limiting inconveniences and sorrows of the ten plagues, including a bloody Nile, frogs, gnats, flies, murrain, boils, hail, locusts, darkness, and the death of Egypt's firstborn.

When Nadab and Abihu, Aaron's sons, took the liberty of exceeding God's rules for sacrifices by offering unholy fire, divine fire devoured them (Lev. 10:1-2). Similarly, 600 years later, when King Uzziah intruded into the priestly office, he was struck with leprosy and consigned to virtual solitary confinement (2 Chron. 26:16-21).

The Israelites in the wilderness, tired of manna, lusted after meat. God gave them their desire to the full, but the result was sickness and misery. The psalmist put it, "He gave them their request, but sent leanness into their soul" (106:15).

Israel insisted on a king like other nations. God warned that a king would conscript their sons into military service, enslave their daughters, and confiscate their grain and cattle. They persisted in their desire and suffered the predicted consequences.

Because Israel repeatedly worshiped false gods and would not heed the prophets who warned them, the Lord removed both kingdoms. In 721 B.C. the northern ten tribes of Israel were taken into captivity by the Assyrians, and around 600 B.C. the southern Judah by the Babylonians. The freedom of disobedience led to exile in strange nations.

Freedom can bring trouble in social situations. Freedom to do one's thing usually brings trouble, especially if it violates the laws of God. The Decalogue provides limits which to exceed means diminishment of the quality of life for the liberty-taker. The child who will not abide by parental authority may become a menace to society, perhaps ending up in a reform school.

If we murder, our liberty will be taken away for years or for life, or perhaps it will mean death. Cain, the first murderer, became a "fugitive and a vagabond" (Gen. 4:14).

The thief may end up doing time. The liar may be trapped in a web of falsehoods. Abraham and Isaac both lied about their wives and lost them temporarily till God revealed the truth to the heathen kings who had kidnapped the wives.

Lack of self-discipline, including love of sleep and dislike of work, leads to the bondage of poverty. The slothful and the spendthrift may be forced to borrow and end up a slave to the lender (see Prov. 12:24; 22:7; 24:30-34.)

The Playboy philosophy brings bondage. A popular philosophy in America today is not some system of thought taught in college, but a method of living popularized under the name *Playboy*. Really nothing new, but a resurrected hedonism, it holds that the pursuit of pleasure is life's highest goal. No one has promoted this cult more than Hugh Hefner, founder of the Playboy enterprises.

We should never forget the prodigal son who thought himself free when he left home to squander his inheritance without restraint on riotous living, but who, finding himself penniless, took a job feeding swine so he could eat the husks they left. His freedom ended in bondage.

Drugs produce slaves. A girl wrote this letter to a columnist:

When I split it was because home was a drag and I thought San Francisco, Los Angeles, and Mexico had a lot in store for me. Well, I was right. They had acid, pot, 13 people in a three-room apartment, venereal disease, and thrift stores where you could buy someone's beat-up jeans for $1. I dug being "free" until I woke up one morning in a Phoenix hospital. You would have thought I learned my lesson but, no, it happened again—an overdose of LSD. After that experience I knew the next time I'd kill myself so I decided to go home.

Thousands of youth think they are free but find themselves hooked, in agony for a fix every few hours, injecting a dirty needle into their veins to get relief. No wonder superstar Johnny Cash, speaking openly about his past addiction to prescription pills, calls drug dependence the equivalent of a mental prison (*Journal News,* Nyack, N.Y., 8/28/85, AP).

And consider alcohol addiction. The damage done our nation by those under the influence of alcohol is stupendous. More than half of all U.S. highway fatalities (50,000 killed in a recent year) are alcohol related. The value of lost labor hours, the cost of rehabilitation, to say nothing of families disrupted and homes lost, all add to the tragedy of alcoholic enslavement. No wonder the writer of Proverbs warns, "Wine gives false courage; hard liquor leads to brawls; what fools men are to let it master them, making them reel drunkenly down the street" (20:1, TLB).

Alcohol promises to turn out men of distinction, but disguises the fact that its user may end up lying in the gutter on the Bowery, evidence that "it biteth like a serpent, and stingeth like an adder" (23:32).

In self-deception a victim may not realize he is enslaved and reject any effort to get help—a poor slave thinking himself free. Such resemble the leaders in Jesus' day, who, resenting His suggestion that they needed liberation, retorted, "We be Abraham's seed, and were never in bondage to any man" (John 8:33). How could they have forgotten their present subjugation to Rome, as well as the slavery in Egypt and the captivities in Assyria and Babylon?

And illicit sex. For decades advocates of sexual freedom have been heralding their cause. Homosexuals have come out of the closet. Every type of sexual perversion is rampant. But liberty has brought bondage. *Newsweek* (February 4, 1985) said that the United States is currently in the grip of an STD (sexually transmitted disease) outbreak of unprecedented proportions. The statistics are scary, indicating that one of every four Americans between 15 and 55 will acquire STD during his or her lifetime. Twenty-seven thousand cases are contracted daily. Ten million people visit medical offices every year for this problem, costing over $2 billion in health-care expense. Some of the new STDs are incurable, often resulting in chronic pain, sterility, abnormal pregnancies, brain-damaged children, and cancer. In the case of AIDS the outcome is almost certain death.

The most enlightened and affluent society in all human history is discovering that we cannot transgress God's laws and not suffer, but that rather, what we sow we also reap. Peter spoke of those who promise liberty, but "they themselves are the servants of corruption, for of whom a man is overcome, of the same is he brought in bondage" (2 Peter 2:19).

When David took liberty with another man's wife, not only did his sin of adultery expand to the murder of a righteous husband and the death of David's infant son, but his example was not lost on his family. When David's son, Amnon, lusted after his half-sister Tamar, he took her—like father, like son. This led to Absalom's murder of Amnon, followed by David's banishment of Absalom, which in turn set the stage for the bitterness that divided David and Absalom. The final blow was the death of Absalom. The scorecard read: three sons dead, daughter raped, family name disgraced. Incidentally, immediately after Amnon violated Tamar, he found himself in the prison of revulsion, for he "hated her exceedingly; so that the hatred wherewith he hated her was greater than the love wherewith he had loved her" (2 Sam. 13:15).

The New York Times reported that Stuyvesant Square, one of New York's finest parks, has become a late-night sexual meeting place for young homosexual men and headquarters for drug dealers. A doctor, who lives nearby and who has witnessed the activity for over a year, says: "I'm amazed these guys are doing their stuff. We know that the highest risk group for AIDS is sexually active homosexual men and intravenous drug users. And those are the guys out there every night in the square. What they're doing is nothing less than suicidal" (October 12, 1985).

Bruce Shelly in *Christian Theology in Plain Language* (Word, p. 58) says fallen men are "like marionettes who have cut their own strings in the hope of finding another way to dance, and finding out too late that without the strings they cannot dance at all."

A fable tells of the fly who, enticed by the spider to enjoy the hospitality of his house, enters only to discover too late that he is hopelessly and fatally enmeshed in the spider's web.

SLAVERY LEADS TO LIBERTY

Tolerance is a pet word today. How bigoted to judge another's view as wrong! Yet these same people are very narrow-minded in so many other areas of life. No room for carelessness exists in the scientific lab where water boils at 212 degrees Fahrenheit at sea level, never at 150 or 189 degrees. The law of gravity is intolerant. If you step off a roof, the law of gravity will not become suddenly lenient and let you float slowly to the ground, but will remain rigid and narrow, dropping you with a jolt to earth.

A secretary after her first day of work complained, "My boss is sort of bigoted. He thinks words can be spelled only one way."

Mathematics is also narrow-minded. Two plus two equals four, not five, nor three.

The phone is narrow-minded. Be a little broad-minded. When dialing miss your desired number by only a digit, and you may reach a party a thousand miles from the person you are calling.

We wish our bus drivers to be narrow, staying within the limited confines of their side of the highway.

When coming in for a landing, we want our pilots to head for that narrow strip of pavement called the runway. A broad-minded touchdown a few yards on either side could bring a tragic crash. Proverbs says, "Turn not to the right hand nor to the left; remove thy foot from evil" (4:27).

The way to heaven is narrow. Somehow people have it in their heads that all roads lead to heaven, but Jesus spoke of a narrow gate and a narrow highway that leads to life. His redemptive work on the cross qualified Him to call Himself "the Way," apart from which exists no entrance to the celestial city. He affirmed, "No man cometh unto the Father, but by Me" (John 14:6).

Billy Graham tells how once when flying from Korea to Japan, his plane encountered a rough snowstorm. He relates: "When we arrived over the airport at Tokyo, the ceiling and visibility were almost zero. The pilot had to make an instrument landing. I sat up in the cockpit with the pilot and watched him sweat it out as he was brought in by ground control approach. I did not wish my pilot nor the air controllers to be broad-minded. I knew that our lives depended on it. Just so, when we come in for a landing in the great airport of heaven, I don't wish any broadmindedness. I want to come in on the beam, and even though I may be considered narrow here, I want to be sure of a safe landing there."

Limits needed. An extensive lead article on AIDS in *Newsweek* (August 12, 1985) surveys the ominous spread and usual incurability of the disease, then makes this remarkable conclusion. The best solution "is a massive educational effort aimed at encouraging the single partner lifestyle and a little restraint in sexual practices" (p. 27). Narrow as it may seem, a return to old-fashioned biblical monogamous marriage is the wisest route to take. Our licentious generation needs to know the glory of freedom that comes from saying no to sexual looseness.

Teenagers, despite their protestations of wanting to do their own thing, really do appreciate limits placed on them by their parents, and find better mental health in knowing the boundaries beyond which they should not go.

Keeping God's laws brings joy. God's restraining laws were never meant to be joy killers but joy-givers. The Ten Commandments were not given to hamper our happiness but to give joy. English psychiatrist Dr. Sydney Sharman, in his book *Psychiatry, the Ten Commandments and You,* suggests that a lifestyle based on the Decalogue reduces immeasurably the vulnerability of an individual to neurotic ill health. Not only does the Decalogue offer a basis of prevention, but also a cure for many of modern man's neuroses. Using several case histories, the psychiatrist illustrates how he has been able to help some patients, not by probing their subconscious, but by confronting the conscious mind with the principles and standards of the Ten Commandments (Dodd, Meade, & Co., New York).

The Lord said, "O that there were such an heart in them, that they would fear Me, and keep all My commandments always, that it might be well with them, and with their children forever!" (Deut. 5:29)

Christianity Today told of a hotel on Florida's Gulf of Mexico whose workers were required to wear shoes when on duty. On the surface the rule seemed restrictive, for the rooms had shag carpets, delightful to the feet and only a few yards from the smooth, white sands. But those who submitted to authority and wore shoes on the job avoided the tiny fragments of undetected broken glass and other clutter left from late night parties, as well as the hard steel bed frames against which it was so easy to stub toes while making beds.

In George Orwell's *Nineteen Eighty-Four* we read: "You know the [Communist] Party slogan: 'Freedom Is Slavery.' Has it ever occurred to you that it is reversible? Slavery is freedom. Alone—free—the human being is always defeated. It must be so, because every human being is doomed to die, which is the greatest of all failures. But if he can make complete, utter submission, if he can escape from his identity, if he can merge himself in the Party so that he is the Party, then he is all-powerful and immortal" (p. 212).

What a poor, inferior, impersonal type of freedom— absorption into the Communist Party—compared to the glorious destiny prepared for the children of God. Among other things, God has predestined us to be conformed to the image of His Son. What honor and liberty! We have been freed from the bonds of keeping the Old Testament law to gain salvation, from all the sacrifices connected therewith, and from the domination of the old nature that keeps dragging us down, so that we are now enabled to live as sons and daughters of God.

The freedom of slavery to Jesus Christ. Paul wrote, "It is for freedom that Christ has set us free. Stand firm, then, and do not let yourselves be burdened again by a yoke of slavery" (Gal. 5:1, NIV). Emancipation by divine grace never leads to libertinism. No more to be enslaved to the works of the flesh, including immorality, idolatry, and intemperance, we are free to walk in the Spirit, be led by the Spirit, and display the fruit of the Spirit (Gal. 5:16-23).

We are not liberated to do our thing, but His. Many think that freedom is life without authority, responsibility, or duties, a rootless lifestyle permitting us to follow the least inclination, notion, whim, or fancy. But the Gospel points to a freedom with purpose. Called unto liberty, we are not to use it for an occasion to the flesh, but by love to serve one another (5:13). When the Israelites were liberated from Egyptian bondage, it was not to take a fishing trip down the Nile, climb the pyramids, buy five pounds of garlic, or go into the manufacture of bricks, but to join God's people on their journey to the Promised Land.

Peter told us to live "as free, and not using your liberty for a cloak of maliciousness, but as the servants of God" (1 Peter 2:16). If we are enslaved to Jesus Christ, we shall be free to walk in His ways. As a medieval leader once wrote, "Love God, and do as you please." Modern political leader Chuck Colson confessed, "I had to go to prison to know what freedom is."

When Dale Evans, the movie star, became a Christian, some friends could not understand the change in her life. She said, "If I could only make them see that Dale Evans has died, and that a willing slave to Christ has been born in her place! When I asked God to make me over, that's exactly what happened."

One of the many names for Christians in the New Testament is *slave*. We have lost the significance of this concept in our day, partly because of the abolition of slavery, and also because of the permissiveness of our day. A slave is one who has a master, who serves this master to the disregard of his own interests, who is on call at all times, and who sometimes suffers thereby. Paul often referred to himself as a servant or slave of Jesus Christ (Rom. 1:1; Phil. 1:1; see *The Living Bible*). In obedience to the orders of his Master, the apostle plodded on from city to city and country to country, even continent to continent. Despite beatings, persecution, imprisonments, stonings, shipwrecks, weariness, pain, hunger, thirst, cold, and nakedness, Paul always abounded in the work of the Lord.

Calling Christ "Master" demands surrender of our own plans in order to do His bidding. Paul wrote, "Though I am free and belong to no man, I make myself a slave to everyone, to win as many as possible" (1 Cor. 9:19, NIV). Then he tells how he became like a Jew, a Gentile, and a weak person, in order to win all these types. He subordinated himself to all men so that by all possible means he might save some (1 Cor. 9:22).

An obscure German monk, Thomas a Kempis, wrote in his monastery diary in the 15th century, "Unless thou deny thyself thou shalt not have perfect liberty."

Years ago in Africa a missionary employed a little boy as his servant. Noticing a scar on the boy's chest a few months later, a mark of ownership in that territory, the missionary reasoned that the boy was a runaway slave. So the missionary found the chief who owned the boy and bought him. He told the lad, "I've purchased your freedom. You can go anywhere you please. No one owns you anymore."

The little boy replied, "I want to belong to you. I don't want to leave you. You set me free." The boy stayed and gave the missionary devoted service, not because he had to, but because he wanted to.

Because Christ purchased our redemption at Calvary, His love constrains us so that we voluntarily become His slaves. The hymnwriter James Small in "I've Found a Friend" put it,

> He drew me with the cords of love,
> And thus He bound me to Him.

NINE
SANCTIFIED WISDOM

Cleverness is folly.
Foolishness is wisdom.

*L*ittle Philip, born with Down's syndrome, attended a third-grade Sunday School class with several eight-year-old boys and girls. Typical of that age, the children did not readily accept Philip with his differences, according to an article in *Leadership* magazine. But because of a creative teacher, they began to care about Philip and accept him as part of the group, though not fully.

The Sunday after Easter the teacher brought Leggs panty-hose containers, the kind that look like large eggs. Each receiving one, the children were told to go outside on that lovely spring day, find some symbol for new life, and put it in the egglike container. Back in the classroom, they would share their new-life symbols, opening the containers one by one in surprise fashion. After running about the church property in wild confusion, the students returned to the classroom and placed the containers on the table. Surrounded by the children, the teacher began to open them one by one. After each one, whether flower, butterfly, or leaf, the class would ooh and aah. Then one was opened, revealing nothing inside. The children exclaimed, "That's stupid. That's not fair. Somebody didn't do their assignment."

Philip spoke up, "That's mine."

"Philip, you don't ever do things right!" the students retorted. "There's nothing there!"

"I did so do it," Philip insisted. "I did do it. It's empty. The tomb was empty!"

Silence followed. From then on Philip became a full member of the class. He died not long afterward from an infection most normal children would have shrugged off. At the funeral this class of eight-year-olds marched up to the altar, not with flowers, but with their Sunday School teacher, each to lay on it an empty panty-hose egg.

Paul wrote, "God hath chosen the foolish things of the world to confound the wise" (1 Cor. 1:27). Many who are wise by this world's standard are foolish in God's sight. Conversely, many considered fools in the sight of the world are considered wise in God's eyes. Paul advised, "If any man among you seemeth to be wise in this world, let him become a fool, that he may be wise. For the wisdom of this world is foolishness with God. For it is written, 'He taketh the wise in their own craftiness.' And again, 'The Lord knoweth the thoughts of the wise, that they are vain' " (1 Cor. 3:18-20).

The ark seemed a symbol of Noah's folly to those who heard him preach and watched him build, but it became the instrument of deliverance of the few wise enough to enter.

The chief priests and scribes, summoned by King Herod to ask where the King of the Jews was to be born, knew the answer, "In Bethlehem of Judea, for thus it is written by the prophet," but these supposed wise men of Israel never found Him. However, the wise men from the East, really heathen, followed the star in the sky and sought Him eagerly and discovered the King (Matt. 2:1-11).

When a preacher in Canada announced by billboard his sermon topic, "The Foolishness of God," he was brought before the court for violating the law against blasphemy.

He explained his theme was a quote from the Bible, "The foolishness of God is wiser than men" which means that the simplest wisdom of God far exceeds the brightest of man's wisdom.

The brilliant Einstein, who neglected to take his glasses with him on a train trip, was unable to read the menu in the dining car. The waiter, ready to take his order, noticed Einstein stumbling over the words. Einstein handed him the menu and asked him to read it to him. The waiter fumbled for a few seconds with the menu, then confessed, "I'm ignorant too, sir." No matter how wise we may be, our wisdom is limited.

If ever inclined to look condescendingly on a retarded person, we should ponder how low our own IQ must be when compared to God's. How stupid we must appear to Him!

CLEVERNESS IS FOLLY

The knowledge explosion doubles our information about every 15 years. Universities abound. Technology advances. Books fly off the press by the million. Despite all our knowledge, worldly wisdom is indeed deficient. Consider five reasons that show the foolishness of worldly wisdom:

● *Worldly wisdom rejects divine truth and believes a lie.* Part of the devil's appeal to Eve was, "If you eat the fruit, you'll be like God, knowing good from evil." Desiring to be made wise, she partook of the forbidden fruit, and gave to Adam. Their rebellion led to spiritual darkness. Paul described the result of the fall in these terms:

> Although they knew God, they neither glorified Him as God nor gave thanks to Him, but their thinking became futile and their foolish hearts were darkened. Although they claimed to be wise, they became fools and exchanged the glory of the immortal God for images made to look like mortal man and birds and

animals and reptiles. . . . They exchanged the truth of God for a lie, and worshiped and served created things rather than the Creator. . . . Because of this, God gave them over to shameful lusts (Rom. 1:21-26, NIV).

Quickly the light of original wisdom faded into the folly of fallen darkness with its idolatry and immorality. How ludicrous for a human to view as a god something which has been chopped down and shaped by man, which has to be carried, which cannot answer a cry for help, cannot lift itself up if fallen over, cannot see, hear or speak, and which can be burned. Yet millions the world over are bewitched by idols. I myself have seen people in the Orient bring offerings of fruit and vegetables and burn toy money to an idol.

Just as ridiculous is the practice of millions in the Western world who would never think of crassly bowing to gods of wood and stone, yet who foolishly give allegiance to gods just as lifeless and empty, which they set up in their hearts: possessions, money, fame, and pleasure.

One who turns from the wisdom of God becomes easy prey for false wisdom like the readings of fortune-tellers, the predictions of astrologers, or the myths of superstition. So-called intelligent people believe it bad luck to walk under a ladder, let their path be crossed by a black cat, or be associated with number 13. Many hotels have no floor marked 13; many airlines have no flight numbered 13.

How well I recall sitting in a graduate philosophy class at the University of Pennsylvania when the mythical island Atlantis came up in a discussion of one of Plato's dialogues. Immediately a brilliant student rushed to defend the reality of this undiscovered, unverified place. Yet this same student did not accept the historicity of the Bible. He denied the truth of God's Word, but easily accepted the existence of what *Webster's New Collegiate Dictionary* defines as "a fabled island that was traditionally placed west of the

Strait of Gibraltar and that was swallowed up by the sea."

At the start of the century our Western universities frequently referred to the God of the Bible. Courses in moral philosophy prominently mentioned the Ten Commandments and the Sermon on the Mount. Today no significant place remains for God in most university classrooms. Science and history omit God as unnecessary. Shared moral values have blurred into pale ghosts on the campus. Wisdom has degenerated into folly.

● *Worldly wisdom cannot explain the riddle of life.* Someone described life as "the predicament that precedes death." Is human wisdom sufficient to solve the mystery of life? Job discovered that worldly wisdom offers no adequate explanation of life's meaning or tragedies. The writer of Ecclesiastes thought wisdom might be the key to the riddle of life, but "perceived that this also is vexation of spirit. For in much wisdom is much grief, and he that increaseth knowledge increaseth sorrow" (1:17-18).

A group of college students sat around a bar, drinking and chatting. How clever they seemed. They knew something about everything: politics' critical problems, international relations, the latest novel, the bestsellers, sports celebrities, and the long-running Broadway plays. But said one observer, "They knew everything except the significance of why they were in that bar."

Where did we come from? Why are we here? Where are we going? How can I be right with God? These questions keep impinging on the human mind and crying out for an answer. Though philosophy tries to give us a comprehensive worldview and a rational explanation of things, man's grasp of reality is too limited. Because we cannot generate enough wisdom to answer the vital questions, the key to the mystery eludes our grasp. This is why God had to give us a revelation from above.

David Hume, empiricist-philosopher, wrote an essay on the sufficiency of the light of nature to meet man's questions. F.W. Robertson, a contemporary clergyman, wrote an essay to establish the opposite conclusion: namely, that the light of nature is insufficient and needs to be supplemented by the light of God. The two men met in the home of a mutual friend one evening in friendly debate. When Hume rose to leave at the end, Robertson took a light to show Hume the way. Hume declined the help, and bowing low, replied, "I find the light of nature always sufficient. Please don't trouble yourself about me." Just then, Hume stumbled over something in the doorway and pitched down the steps into the dark street. Robertson ran after him with his light, and holding it above the prostrate skeptic, whispered softly, "You had better have a little light from above, friend Hume."

Because of the insufficiency of human wisdom, God has given us a revelation, which, though not answering all our questions, does give enough light to satisfy our intellectual and moral needs. Christian truth, though not discoverable by human reasoning, is not anti-intellectual. Rather, once accepted, God's revelation is found to be intellectually respectable and defensible. Wisdom that disregards divine revelation is folly.

● *Worldly wisdom makes stupid predictions.* The book *The World's Worst Predictions* lists some of history's all-time prophetic goofs. King George II said in 1773 that the American colonies had little stomach for revolution.

An official of the White Star Line, speaking of the firm's newly built flagship, the *Titantic*, launched in 1912, declared that the ship was unsinkable.

In 1939 *The New York Times* said the problem with TV was that people had to glue their eyes to a screen, and that the average American wouldn't have time for it.

An English astronomy professor said in the early 19th century that rail travel at high speed would be impossible because passengers would suffocate.

Back in 1955 a group of national leaders made predictions about what 1975 would bring, then sealed them in a time capsule in the Prudential Insurance Company's main office in Minneapolis, opening them in June 1975. Most were unfulfilled. For example, "By 1975 there will be little inflation." Also, "A telephone in nearly every room in the house will be considered essential." Also, "The car of 1975 will bear little resemblance to those of today." There was little difference between the models of '55 and '75.

● *Worldly wisdom does not produce virtue.* Socrates said that knowledge is virtue. But knowledge does not necessarily lead to virtuous action. Alexander the Great, who died of intemperance at 33, had for his teacher Aristotle, one of the world's all-time great philosophers. Nero had for his teacher the wise Seneca. Chou-en-lai, longtime premier of China, became one of the founders of the Chinese Communist Party while a student in France. It is estimated that half of China's Communist leaders in the early years turned to Communism while attending U.S. universities. The two most literate nations when World War II started were Germany and Japan. The worldly wisdom of our universities indeed seems deficient.

One dean of students, noting the large number of college students indulging in petty thievery from neighborhood supermarkets, observed, "It makes you wonder what these kids are getting from their education."

A young woman with an M.A. in marketing was found deliberately soiling a dress so she could mark it down and buy it herself at a bargain price.

An office worker with an advanced degree from a leading university was caught pilfering from the cashbox. When confronted, she snapped back, "There's no such thing as right or wrong. If you're caught, it's wrong. Otherwise, it's right."

The New York Academy of Medicine Library reported many parts of pages missing from expensive volumes. Using a common razor, medical student-surgeons with careful incisions had sliced out important copy for their files or research papers.

Former Mayor Curley of Boston said that when serving

time in federal prison he learned that practically every college in the country, including Harvard, Yale, and Columbia, was represented among the inmate population. One day as Curley walked into the prison library, a kindly fellow asked if Curley remembered him. It turned out that Curley addressed MIT's graduation class when this man received his degree.

Education which rejects Christian philosophy undermines any firm foundation for good behavior. Much of modern education denies the reality of the supernatural, rejects changeless truth and moral absolutes, and spurns the relevance of historic Christian theism for the crucial problems of thought and life. Yet most of the first hundred colleges and universities in our nation were founded with the Christian faith as the unifying core of their curriculum. This ideal has long since faded from academia.

● *Worldly wisdom leads to foolish views and twisted values.* The Bible calls fools those who deny in word or practice the existence of God (Ps. 14:1), fail to believe the biblical record (Luke 24:25-27), depart from the simplicity of the Gospel by adding works to faith (Gal. 3:1-3), or despise parental or divine instruction (Prov. 12:1; 15:5, 20, 32-33).

Jesus called a certain rich man a fool for several reasons (Luke 12:16-20). The man forgot who had given him the power to accumulate riches. He treated his wealth as though it were his own: "my fruits, my barns, my goods." He forgot the poor around him. He forgot the fragility of life, counting on many years to live, not realizing he would die that night. He laid up wealth for himself, and forgot he was poor toward God. How many do we all know who today are accumulating wealth and ignoring God?

The world's vaunted wisdom is often stupidity from a divine viewpoint. On the other hand, what may seem foolish to man may turn out to be part of God's great wisdom.

FOOLISHNESS IS WISDOM

What seems foolish to us may show the wisdom of God. A tired farmer sat under a walnut tree to escape the noonday heat. Looking at his pumpkin vines, he thought, "How strange for God to put such big, heavy pumpkins on a vine so frail that it trails on the ground." Then looking up at the tree above him, he thought, "How strange that God puts such small walnuts on such a big tree with branches so strong they could hold a man." Just then a breeze dislodged a walnut. The farmer wondered no more at God's strangeness as he rubbed his head ruefully. "It's a good thing there wasn't a pumpkin up there instead of a walnut!"

Divine wisdom uses foolish things. God used Moses' rod, a slender piece of wood, roughly five feet long, to make the Red Sea part for the deliverance from Egyptian bondage, as well as to perform other miracles.

Citizens of Jericho, observing the Israelites march silently around their walls once a day for six days, must have been curious about this seemingly absurd military exercise. But the wisdom of God became evident on the seventh day when the walls fell down and the city was captured.

God used Balaam's donkey to drive truth into the prophet's head. Naaman thought it illogical to dip into the muddy Jordan when his own Syrian rivers were superior. But the ridiculous turned out to be the remedy.

God used ravens to feed Elijah. To bring back a backslidden Jonah, God used a fish, the wind, a plant, and a worm. Jesus used a fish with a coin in its mouth to pay a tax, and a colt on which to ride into Jerusalem.

God often uses strange things to accomplish His purposes. During a storm on the *Mayflower's* Atlantic crossing, one of the main supporting deck beams cracked. Disaster loomed, since normally a ship would have nothing to correct the situation, especially on a stormy ocean. However, the Pilgrims had on board just the thing to prop up the deck—a giant screw. No one knows why it was on board, perhaps as a part of an old-fashioned printing press, or as a jack for houses they would build. This unlikely screw was placed under the beam for support the rest of the voyage.

Paul breaks out in doxology, "O the depth of the riches both of the wisdom and knowledge of God! How unsearchable are His judgments, and His ways past finding out!" (Rom. 11:33)

Divine wisdom shines through the foolishness of the cross. No human could ever have dreamed up the story of God redeeming us through the death of His Son on the cross. The ignominious death of a cross was reserved for criminals, foreigners, and slaves. For anyone to die that disdainful death and then be declared Saviour and Lord was unthinkable. Paul wrote, "The preaching of the cross is to them that perish foolishness" (1 Cor. 1:18). The word *foolishness* gives us our English word *moron*. The Gospel was "moron stuff."

In the early years of his large crusades, Billy Graham was under consideration by a California university as a possible speaker. Though the evangelist was ultimately invited, one professor said, "A lecture by Graham would be an offense to the intellect." But since that time Graham has become a welcome speaker at the world's leading universities such as Oxford and Cambridge; even so, many unbelieving intellectuals still feel his message offensive.

To unbelievers the cross may be foolishness, but to those who believe it has become the power of God to meet the need of fallen man by giving forgiveness and a dynamic to direct his life into righteous channels. People in all ages and cultures have found pardon, strength, and hope through this seemingly foolish message. Through it, nasty people have been made kind, resentful people have become forgiving, alcoholics have been freed from their habit, and lawbreakers have become law-abiding citizens.

When Paul came to the wisdom-loving Corinthians, he

came not with enticing words of wisdom, declaring, "For I determined not to know anything among you, save Jesus Christ, and Him crucified" (1 Cor. 2:2). When he preached the Gospel in Athens, they called him a babbler. Yet this old, old story has had a wondrous attraction for people through the centuries, and for literally millions today who never tire of hearing it over and over.

Divine wisdom is often hidden from the so-called wise and revealed to the simple. The new resident in the housing development didn't lose any time letting people know he was an atheist. Meeting a new neighbor for the first time, he would introduce himself, mention that he was a research scientist, then say, "There's no need to believe in the supernatural. For example, we can make rain now. We just send a fellow up in a plane. He drops some chemicals on a cloud, and presto—it rains."

To his utter amazement one day, a neighbor's eight-year-old daughter piped up, "Who made the cloud?"

Jesus prayed, "I thank Thee, O Father, Lord of heaven and earth, because Thou hast hid these things from the wise and prudent, and hast revealed them unto babes" (Matt. 11:25). The Lord did not mean that intellectual acumen invariably prevents faith, but that it is unnecessary. The most unlearned can grasp saving truth regarding Christ. Lack of learning does not disqualify. He was saying, in effect, "You don't have to be in *Who's Who* to know what's what."

Jesus often hid things from wise skeptics and learned unbelievers, but revealed them to His simple, unpretentious disciples. For example, the Pharisees asked for a sign, but He gave them none except that of the Prophet Jonah (Matt. 12:38ff). But when His disciples asked for a sign, His answer covered the space of two chapters (Matt. 24–25). The schooled Pharisees did not believe His deity, but fisherman Simon Peter understood this truth (Matt. 16:16-18).

When Jesus healed a man born blind, the Pharisees just

would not accept the miracle, despite incontrovertible evidence. He commented, "For judgment I am come into this world, that they which see not might see; and that they which see might be made blind" (John 9:39). The blind man came to see both physically and spiritually, whereas the Pharisees who claimed to have the light were shown to be spiritually blind.

Though the learned Sanhedrin perceived the apostles as "unlearned and ignorant men," Peter's defense made them marvel and admit the disciples had imbibed the wisdom of Jesus (Acts 4:13). When the same council disputed with Stephen, they could not "resist the wisdom and spirit by which he spake" (6:9-10). The early church was described as "not many wise men after the flesh" (1 Cor. 1:26). Yet they possessed true wisdom.

A part-time local preacher, a shepherd from the hills, was invited to say a few words at a dinner sponsored by a scientific society in a small town in northern England. Though he keenly felt his intellectual limitations, he wished to give a witness. So rising slowly, he began, "Gentlemen, I am not versed in your sciences, but am a plain, simple man. I don't know much about the stars, but I do know the Bright and Morning Star. I don't know much about botany, but I do know the Lily of the Valley and the Rose of Sharon. I don't know much about the major philosophies of the world, but I do know Him who is the source of all wisdom. I don't know much about geography, but I do know my way to the cross of Calvary."

The source of true wisdom. The way God wants us to live is found in His book of directions, the Bible. Men may deem God's ways foolish, but in reality they are the paths of wisdom. Though God's truth is spread through all 66 Bible books, Proverbs especially is known as the wisdom book. To follow the paths of wisdom leads to happiness, protection, abundant life. To reject God's wisdom leads to disaster, calamity, distress.

A Christian philosophy centers in the Bible as God's

revelation and authority in matters of faith and practice, applies the relevancy of God to every area of learning, and requires a personal encounter with Jesus Christ "in whom are hid all the treasures of wisdom and knowledge" (Col. 2:3). Only after he was born again could Chuck Colson comprehend the true nature of things. In his book *Loving God* (Zondervan), the former special counsel to President Nixon wrote of his preconversion days:

> I was blind. Indeed, only in the "breakdown of power" did I finally understand both it and myself. For my view of life was through such narrow openings as the elegantly draped windows of the White House, and my vistas were of lush green lawns, manicured bushes, and proud edifices housing the corridors of power. But looking at the world from the underside through the bars of a dark prison cage and the barbed wire of forced confinement, I could, for the first time, really *see* (p. 170).

Every spring break thousands of college students who are supposedly pursuing wisdom indulge in the folly of drunkenness and immorality on Florida and Caribbean beaches. Every three years between Christmas and New Year's Day 18,000 students gather at the Urbana Inter-Varsity Missionary Convention on the University of Illinois campus. As many as half the participants in one conference testified that they had made a Christian commitment in the three preceding years. These were the students who discovered that the fear of the Lord is the beginning of wisdom.

Just before William Jennings Bryan went off to college for the first time, his father called him into his study. Expecting to hear a lecture on the dangers of sin and the weaknesses of youth, young William was surprised when his father merely asked him to agree to read the Book of Proverbs through once a month for a year. Byran promised and kept his word. Later in life after gaining eminence in law and politics, he looked back at his father's request as a major factor in his success. Through reading Proverbs 12 times that critical year, he received wisdom to make practical decisions that avoided pitfalls, especially that of choosing foolish friends.

Many people read a chapter of Proverbs daily. With 31 chapters in the book, they read Proverbs through entirely every month. If we wish to grow in true wisdom, we must not only read and re-read this volume of proverbial wisdom, but also become familiar with the entire Bible which speaks of the God of wisdom, Christ who is made unto us wisdom, and the Holy Spirit who applies divine wisdom to our lives.

It's the entrance of God's Word that gives light. The psalmist said, "The testimony of the Lord is sure, making wise the simple" (19:7).

TEN
BOTTOM-LINE WEALTH

Rich yet poor.
Poor yet rich.

Newsweek cover story called 1984 "The Year of the Yuppie." Yuppies—young urban professionals—were described as aging hippies or civilized rebels who tried drugs and all those other things but who have been transformed by middle- and upper-class values into the sons or daughters their parents wanted them to be.

Yuppies are convinced money is the essence of all good. One frank Yuppie confessed she would be "comfortable with $200,000 a year." Another said, "I've started to live the American dream. I want a business. I want to be rich. I want to have more money than I can spend. I want a Jaguar and maybe a quarter-of-a-million-dollar house." Conspicuous possessions, exotic restaurants, $600-a-month health clubs, frequent vacation trips, fine wines, and no children—all reflect the thinking of a group that defines itself by what it owns. Emblazoned across the shirt of one Yuppie was a telling motto, "The one who dies with the most toys wins."

Yuppies and all who think like them need to consider a statement made many years ago by the poet Rudyard Kipling. At a McGill University commencement address in

Montreal, Canada, he warned students against an over-concern for money, position, or fame. "Someday you will meet a man who cares for none of these things. Then you will know how poor you really are," Kipling declared.

Yes, it's possible to be rich yet poor.

Poor Little Rich Boy is the title of a book on the life of millionaire Colonel Robert R. McCormick. Gloria Vanderbilt was called "poor little rich girl" in the June 1985 United Airlines magazine.

The Bible suggests that some poor in this world's goods may be rich in God's value system, and thus be the rich poor. Proverbs says, "There is that maketh himself rich, yet hath nothing; there is that maketh himself poor, yet hath great riches" (13:7). "Better is a little with righteousness than great revenues without right" (16:8). It's better to have a dry morsel with quietness, than to have a house full of food with strife (17:1).

A tax assessor, as the story goes, came to the home of a poor Christian worker to determine the amount of taxes he would have to pay. "I'm very wealthy," the Christian replied. "First, I have everlasting life. Second, I have a home reserved for me in heaven, also an inheritance that can never be lost. Then I have peace in my heart, and joy unspeakable. I have a loving, faithful wife. The Bible says her worth is far above precious stones. Then I have healthy, obedient children. I have loyal friends. I have comfort for my sorrows and strength for my burdens. And above all, I have a Saviour, Jesus Christ, who supplies all my needs."

The auditor closed his book. "Truly you are a very rich man, but your assets are not subject to taxation." It's possible to be poor yet rich.

RICH YET POOR

Someone wrote: "Money can buy a bed but not sleep, books but not intelligence, food but not appetite, finery but not beauty, a house but not a home, medicine but not health, luxuries but not culture, fun but not happiness." The power of money is generally limited to tangible objects, but it's often powerless to buy intangible values.

An English newspaper offered a prize for the best definition of money. The winner wrote, "Money is the universal passport to everywhere except heaven, and the universal provider for everything except happiness." Some things the rich cannot buy. Sometimes money loses its might and turns mighty mute.

The rich are often poor in health. Money cannot guarantee the ability to enjoy food. A young businessman strove hard to climb the ladder of success, often limiting his noon lunch hour to half an hour or less. He grabbed a sandwich, though he yearned for something more satisfying eaten under more relaxed conditions. Promoted to a top executive position, he had a two-hour lunch period. But by that time he had worked so hard that his doctor limited him to a toothpick and water for lunch, so the story goes!

Ecclesiastes says, "A man to whom God hath given riches, wealth, and honor, so that he wanteth nothing for his soul of all that he desireth, yet God giveth him not power to eat thereof, but a stranger eateth it" (6:2).

Money cannot buy freedom from disease. Financial resources may help prevent illness through proper medicine, and even in the hour of sickness provide the best medical and hospital care. Yet money cannot keep physical malady fully and finally away. Nor can all the money in the world effect a cure. Mrs. William Wrigley, Jr., who outlived her multimillionaire husband by more than a quarter century, spent the last 11 years of her life in a coma. In regard to conscious enjoyment of wealth, she was virtually a penniless pauper.

Nor can money buy exemption from death. The rich fool, his barns filled with plenty, told his soul to take its ease. But that night death came and spoiled all he had worked for (Luke 12:18-21). All the money in the world cannot keep the hearse from someday driving up to our door.

The rich are often poor in security. A few years ago, just before the final push by the Vietcong against South Vietnam, a man named Hong Van Hoanh was one of South Vietnam's elite, a dapper man of prominence, prestige, privilege, and plenty. He owned a thriving business, had a dozen children, two large homes, four cars, and seven servants. Two weeks later he was a refugee, impoverished, dazed by the sudden rush of history that swept him, in just 13 days, from a life of luxury in Saigon to a sweltering little tent at Eglin Air Force Base, Florida. Forty-four-year-old Mr. Hong stood gaunt and haggard in his tent beneath two bare light bulbs, glancing around at his wife and the seven younger children he was able to bring along, as well as surveying the meager remnants of their former life crammed into suitcases and shopping bags.

When General MacArthur and his troops retreated from Corregidor in World War II, stacks of U.S. currency had to be left behind. To keep the money from falling into enemy hands, soldiers burned new $100 bills. As the carton of bills melted into a blackened, burnt, shapeless mass, money never looked cheaper. Though the soldiers had "money to burn," the currency was powerless to stave off military defeat.

When a boy was kidnapped and held for a large ransom, his father exclaimed his wish to be back earning only $100 a week, instead of possessing so much money, for then his boy would never have become the target of kidnappers. Riches do not prevent kidnappers but rather they invite them.

The rich are often poor in happiness. A wealthy Persian lamented, "I never eat, nor drink, nor sleep with any more pleasure now than when I was poor. By having much, I merely gained this—I have the trouble taking care of all the demands made on me."

A rich English nobleman complained he was never so

happy as when living in a simple apartment. Now the huge mansion was a drag on him. His long train of servants were more his masters than his servants. The discharging of heavy duties related to his vast property hampered him enough to remove the sweetness of life. An English millionaire said, "I am a poor rich man burdened with money, but I have nothing else." He died later while signing a check for a large sum.

Money cannot bring happiness in the hour of tragedy. Does an incurably sick man hug his bankbook to his heart? Does a dying millionaire pray to his stocks, bonds, and money markets? Do $100 bills make the best handkerchiefs to dry one's tears? Money which looms large in the hour of smooth sailing dwindles to little consequence in the face of death. Money, like cargo, is often mentally thrown overboard in time of storm.

The rich are often poor in family relationships. A man whose greed drove his wife and children out of his life lay dying in a hospital. To a visiting minister he confessed, "I don't have a friend on earth. I have thousands of dollars, but dollars cannot buy love."

Dr. Gilbert Beers, a senior editor of *Christianity Today*, once asked the mortician at Forest Lawn Cemetery in California what was the most expensive funeral he ever had there. The mortician told of a man so embittered at his ex-wife and children that he left them nothing, but provided $200,000 (which would have equaled half a million today) for his own ostentatious farewell. A bronze casket and beautiful rose window and other costs used up $100,000. What to do with the other $100,000? The solution was orchids. How many attended this spectacular event? Only three (*Christianity Today*, May 7, 1985).

The rich are often poor in godly character. Simon the Sorcerer, amazed at the wonders performed by Peter, offered to buy this power with money. The apostles soundly rebuked him, "Thy money perish with thee, because thou hast thought that the gift of God may be purchased with money" (Acts 8:20). The sin of trying to buy spiritual power with cash has been named after this sorcerer— *simony.*

The filling and fruit of the Holy Spirit have no connection with money. Holiness and growth in grace are not produced by payment of dollars. No sales counter exists where one can exchange a $50 bill for unselfishness, patience, long-suffering, gentleness, self-control, meekness, or love of enemies. Strong Christian character is the result of diligent application to the means God has placed at our disposal. It does not flourish overnight, much less is it bought with money, but it grows through consistent consecration.

Some church members think that a regular gift to the church or missions excuses them from active participation in home and foreign missions. But the deeper life can never be replaced or replenished by dollars and cents. The church of Laodicea heard this scathing evaluation, "Thou sayest, I am rich, and increased with goods, and have need of nothing; and knowest now that thou art wretched, and miserable, and poor, and blind, and naked" (Rev. 3:17). Rich yet poor.

The rich cannot buy heaven. Though money is indispensable in buying a home on earth, it cannot buy a home in heaven. On the contrary, the love of money may keep a person from heaven, as it did the rich young ruler. "It's easier," said Jesus, "for a camel to go through the eye of a needle, than for a rich man to enter into the kingdom of God" (Matt. 19:24). Some rich people have bought tickets to most major countries, but at life's end they will be unable to buy their passage to heaven. They will be like the old Indian chief who went to buy a train ticket. He offered wampum and beads in payment. When the agent refused him a ticket, he was very indignant. He protested, "I'm the richest man in the tribe, and I can't buy a ticket over your railroad." Though rich at home, he was poor in the outside world. Currency of this earth is unacceptable for payment on heavenly homes.

Money cannot buy forgiveness of sins. "Ye are not re-deemed with corruptible things, as silver and gold . . . but with the precious blood of Christ" (1 Peter 1:18). Respite from judgment, remission of sins, residence in heaven—these cannot be claimed over the counters of commerce even with all the world's capital. The invitation to heaven bears no price tag. "Ho, everyone that thirsteth, come ye to the waters and he that hath no money; come ye, buy, and eat; yea, come, buy wine and milk without money and without price" (Isa. 55:1). As an old hymn says,

> Count your many blessings; money cannot buy
> Your reward in heaven, nor your home on high.

A well-to-do but spiritually bankrupt businessman was showing a friend around his estate. From a second-floor balcony the owner remarked, "As far as you can see to the north, that's mine." Then pointing west, south, and east, he made the same claim, "That's mine." Quietly his friend, pointing upward, asked, "And how much do you own up there?" How reminiscent of Jesus' remark about the rich farmer, whose contemplation of his well-filled barns was cut short by death, "so is he that layeth up treasure for himself, and is not rich toward God" (Luke 12:21).

The poverty of some rich persons is summed up in a young woman's remark about her father, a self-made, substantial, and important businessman: "My father has everything he thought he wanted. He has accumulated two houses, carefully equipped with burglar alarms and special locks, three cars and a pickup truck for the country place which has a full-time watchman. He also owns some costly furniture and all the latest gadgets. He also has ulcers. Actually he is a prisoner of his own possessions, a pauper for money's sake."

It's better to have our wealth in heaven, than our heaven in wealth. The latter indicates, not wealth, but poverty.

POOR YET RICH
In a group of men at dinner, someone tossed out the cliché, "Money can buy anything." A wealthy merchant impulsively offered $500 to anyone who could name just four things which money could not buy. Doubting that anyone could meet the challenge, he smiled confidently when one man took his pencil and scribbled four short lines. The challenger passed the paper to the merchant, who glanced at it carelessly first, then gave it a more concentrated look. Within a minute he took out his checkbook to keep his promise. The paper listed these four items: a baby's smile; youth after it is gone; the love of a good woman; entrance into heaven.

You don't have to be rich to enjoy the simple joys of life. A popular song title of past years declared, "The Best Things in Life Are Free." Every day God paints a beautiful sunrise and breath-taking sunset in His unique, unsurpassable brilliance. Could man create such works of art, he would fence them in and charge admission to see them. But God gives performances twice daily without cost.

John Calvin, who disdained riches but who delighted in nature's beauty, wrote in the preface of Olivetan's New Testament in 1535, "The little singing birds are singing of God; the beasts cry unto Him; the elements are in awe of Him; the mountains echo His name; the waves and fountains cast their glances at Him; grass and flowers laugh out to Him." The glories of creation are observable by the poor and unpurchasable by the gold of earth.

Many poor have divine wisdom which is clearly stated to be superior to silver and gold (Prov. 3:13-14). An honorable reputation is wealth available to the poor. "A good name is rather to be chosen than great riches" (22:1).

Also, numerous poor possess the riches of health. The lame man who begged alms at the temple received something superior to silver and gold when healed physically and spiritually through the instrumentality of Peter and John. A contented, godly woman said to her husband, "We have our health; someday we may have money."

When a rich man gets his enjoyment from the simple virtues of life, he is doubly rich. According to *The Wall Street Journal,* a 1985 survey of thousands of millionaires reveals them as a group who derive pleasure from the simple values. They work long hours, take little vacation, have long marriages, drive four-door American sedans or Volvos with no chrome, or rattle along in old station wagons. Four of ten of their wives work. Only 1 in 10 owns a yacht, and a mere 1 in 20 owns a plane. Only about half have a second home. The key word for most of them is work, about 75 hours a week. The article concluded that these rich are a painfully disciplined lot and some of the happiest in the world. The items that make for bottom-line wealth are available to the poor.

A happy family is better than jewels. A visitor, seeing Bishop Waltham's large family, remarked, "These are they that make the poor man rich." Though today's economy makes the expense of rearing a family sky-high, the psalmist said, "Children are an heritage of the Lord . . . happy is the man that hath his quiver full of them" (127:3, 5).

A statue in Forest Lawn Memorial Park in California called *Mother's Jewels* takes its name from a story of a Roman matron named Cornelia, honored mother whose sons performed outstanding service for their country. When a visitor asked to see her jewels, she called her sons and exclaimed, "These are my jewels."

Two brothers, owners of a successful business, were offered a controlling interest in a new company if they would take it over. They refused on the following grounds: "We are men with growing children. We are also active in our church. We are making a comfortable living with time left to give our evenings to our families and to our church. If we take over this new company, the longer hours will leave little or no time for church and children. We have decided that we cannot sacrifice our families, our health, and the Lord's work to make more money we can survive without." These brothers could have become rich, but they chose a more meaningful and lasting bottom-line wealth.

A right relationship with God is better than earthly wealth. Real riches consist not in having, but in being and in doing—being right with God through the redemptive work of Jesus Christ, and in doing His will. Not what we have, but what we are, makes life rich.

Many who possess much have downcast hearts. A person free of condemnation has inward wealth, because he is reconciled to God. He has Christ, the Bread of Life, to fill the vacuum of his empty heart. He has a continuous spiritual feast through meditation in the Bible, prayer, fellowship, giving, service, and soul-winning.

Reading the evening paper in their palatial home in New York City, a wealthy woman said to her husband, "I hear they're doing a good work down at the McAuley Water Street Mission. Let's go down and help them." They found the mission full, so they sat at the rear. As they listened to the testimonies of the men who one by one told how God had rescued them, a new world opened to the rich couple. Finally, the wife whispered, "I guess they'll have to help us instead of our helping them. They've got something we haven't." Later when the invitation was given, this finely dressed pair responded and knelt at the altar in the sawdust beside drunken men and outcasts of the waterfront. There they found real riches.

Matthew Henry wrote, "I would think it a greater happiness to gain one soul to Christ than mountains of silver and gold to myself."

Consider the rich man and Lazarus. Jesus told a story about a rich man and a poor man. The rich man wore expensive clothes. He also ate well. His crime was not wearing fine clothes and eating elegantly but forgetting the beggar at his gate. In the midst of his plenty, he put the poor fellow out of his mind.

Jesus didn't give us the rich man's name, but He did give us the name of the beggar—Lazarus. Every day, probably too ill to walk, the poor fellow was put at the rich man's gate. His body was full of sores which the dogs licked. Was he too weak to ward them off, or did they soothe his irritated skin in sympathy? In his hunger he ate bits of food discarded from the rich man's table.

What a contrast! The rich man clothed in purple and fine linen; the beggar covered with sores. The rich man eating sumptuously; the beggar existing on crumbs. Servants attending the rich man; dogs, the beggar's company.

A man's financial condition is no indication of his spiritual state. True riches depend not on what's in our pockets, but what's in our hearts. It would soon be evident who was the rich man and who was the beggar. The so-called rich man would soon discover that "it's best to go to heaven in rags than to hell in embroidery."

Not surprisingly, since he lacked regular nourishment and medical care, Lazarus died first. Probably there was no funeral, no pallbearers, no coffin, no mourners. Poor fellow—not a friend in the world. But if only they could have seen his real funeral as angels conducted him to his blissful destination. The poor beggar was really the rich one.

Then it was the rich man's turn to die, perhaps on sheets of silk, his head on a soft pillow, in a palatial mansion. The pallbearers were the elite of the community. Banks of flowers, crowds, and lavish eulogies featured the extravaganza. But the rich man was really the poor one. A minute after death what good were all his expensive clothes, tasty food, and money? In a place of torment, he couldn't get water. The rich man became the beggar, asking not for a barrel, nor for a bottle, but for one tiny drop. The Lord answered, in effect, "You were rich during your life, and you didn't help the poor. Now you are poor, and you will not be enriched."

And Zaccheus. Zaccheus, a sort of commissioner of internal revenue in the Jericho district, was rich. But the Bible says he was lost. Not only was he lost to God, but he was lost to himself for not living a useful and productive life, and he was lost to the people of Jericho who shunned him because of dishonest practices that funneled shekels into his own pocket. Rich yet poor.

But one day Jesus invited Himself to Zaccheus' home for a meal. Zaccheus accepted the invitation immediately and joyfully. To demonstrate the reality of his conversion, he openly promised to give half of his goods to the poor, and to repay fourfold those he had defrauded. By nightfall, after he gave half of his wealth to the poor and made restitution, his assets were considerably depleted. Rich in the morning, poorer at night. Really, the reverse was true. In the morning he had been spiritually poor; at night, rich indeed, possessing peace, satisfaction, noble purpose, clean conscience, and assurance from Jesus' lips, "This day is salvation come to this house" (Luke 19:1-10).

Remember the church at Smyrna? The believers at Smyrna, one of the seven churches of Asia Minor, suffered great persecution which reduced them to poverty (Rev. 2:8-9). The worst was yet to come, involving imprisonment and martyrdom. A strange compliment is paid to this church. After mentioning its poverty, the writer adds, "But thou art rich." How were they rich? They had the presence and understanding of Christ who also experienced poverty and persecution. Their conviction that God would never fail them made them faithful unto death, earning for them the crown of life (2:10). Their poverty led to greater riches.

Incidentally, a person poor in this world's goods can through material sharing and spiritual example be a source of blessing to fellow believers. Paul described such a person as "poor, yet making many rich; as having nothing, and yet possessing all things" (2 Cor. 6:10).

A rich man who lived in a mansion heard someone singing in the street out front, "I'm the child of a King." At first he could see no one, but finally detected the source—a manhole. Peering down, his eyes becoming more accustomed to the dark below, he made out the form of a workman in muddy overalls, face grimy, shoveling away as he repaired some underground pipes. As he dug, he kept singing over and over, "I'm a child of the King . . . with Jesus my Saviour, I'm a child of the King."

The rich man couldn't understand. He didn't know the Gospel with its power to adopt sinners into the family of the King of kings. He, the wealthy, was really poor, while the common laborer was really rich.

James wrote, "Has not God chosen those who are poor in the world to be rich in faith and heirs of the kingdom which He has promised to those who love Him?" (2:5, RSV)

Thus, our goal in life should not be the accumulation of earthly assets. Rather we should aim at building our wealth in those areas that count for time and eternity, and thus be rich toward God.

ELEVEN
SUPERNATURAL STRENGTH

Strong yet weak.
Strength made perfect in weakness.

Traditionally, short men are considered underdogs in sports, movies, and politics. Professor Jack M. Feldman of the University of Florida says: "This bias is a basic response, like the process that happens when we look at an optical illusion. Traits like leadership, bravery, and masculinity are expected to be more so in tall men."

But the so-called John Wayne image is slowly changing. With many of today's celebrities well below the six-foot mark once required to qualify as a big, strong guy, focus has shifted from height to characteristics like ability, achievement, and attitude. We are surprised to learn how we overestimate the height of many stars. Dustin Hoffman is 5′ 6″; Mel Brooks, 5′ 4″. Today's movie audiences don't seem to mind when their screen idols only reach the leading lady's chin. Minimum height requirements for many jobs like prison guards and firemen have been lowered in many states.

Perhaps no one has done more recently to boost the ego of the under six-foot crowd than quarterback Doug Flutie. Though listed at 5′ 9¾″, he was measured just before turning pro at the Hula Bowl at just 5′ 8″. Many questioned whether he was tall and strong enough to play football with the big pros. But he won the Heisman Trophy and a five-year $7 million contract with the New Jersey Generals, the highest annual salary in pro football. He played well in the big man's league till sidelined by an injury halfway through the season. Now, as this is written, he has the challenge of making it in the National Football League with the Chicago Bears.

God's upside-down kingdom reverses our superficial equation of tall with tough, and short with shakiness. In God's evaluation, often the strong are really weak, and the weak often strong. Man's strength may fizzle into weakness, whereas God can show Himself strong through human weakness. We may be too big for God to use, but we cannot be too small.

STRONG YET WEAK

The Lord warned against trust in horses and chariots, and in strong horsemen instead of looking unto the all-powerful God of Israel before whom all will fall (Isa. 31:1-3). The Lord came to Elijah, not in the strong wind that breaks rocks in pieces, nor in the earthquake, nor fire, but in a still small voice (1 Kings 19:11-12).

Dr. Paul Tournier wrote in *The Strong and the Weak:*

It is impossible to write about the strong and the weak without underlining, in all its fullness, the way Jesus Christ completely upset the scale of human values. Open the Bible, and this is what you see: He was severe and implacable with the strong, the powerful, the virtuous, the rich, and the great ones of this world. Not, indeed, in any spirit of animosity, but in order to smash that confidence in themselves which closed to them the road to humility (Westminster, p. 243).

Though Tournier went on to say that for the weak, the

poor, the sick, the repentant, the despairing, the Lord had only tenderness, He did emphasize His severity on those who felt their own strength sufficient.

The Lord rendered the giants of Canaan weak. The Children of Israel failed to enter the Promised Land because of their fear of reported giants there, in whose sight they regarded themselves as grasshoppers. When the next generation stood poised to enter the Promised Land, the Lord assured them:

> Hear, O Israel: Thou art to pass over Jordan this day, to go in to possess nations greater and mightier than thyself, cities great and fenced up to heaven, a people great and tall, the children of the Anakims, whom thou knowest, and of whom thou hast heard say, who can stand before the children of Anak! Understand therefore this day, that the Lord thy God is He which goeth over before thee; as a consuming fire He shall destroy them, and He shall bring them down before thy face; so shalt thou drive them out, and destroy them quickly (Deut. 9:1-3).

The Canaanite giants became grasshoppers, and the Israelite grasshoppers became giants.

The Lord rendered Samson weak. Samson was strong, able to kill a lion with bare hands, pull down a city's gateposts, tie the tails of 300 foxes together, and set them afire to destroy enemy fields. But though a physical giant, he was a moral pygmy. Apart from the power of God he was weak. Succumbing to the wiles of a woman, he was blinded and mocked (Jud. 14–16). Not till in weakness he called on the Lord, "Strengthen me," did he have the might to pull down the pillars of a house and slay more than all he had slain in his life (16:28).

The Lord rendered Goliath weak. When young David went out to challenge the towering Goliath, he found King Saul's armor too heavy and clumsy. So putting it all off, he chose just five smooth stones from the brook for his sling. Goliath came at David with sword, spear, and shield, trusting his own strength, but David came in the name and power of God, striking the giant in his one vulnerable spot. Then standing over fallen Goliath, he took the brute's sword and decapitated him. Goliath wasn't the only giant who fell. Samuel mentions four men of great stature slain by David or his servants (2 Sam. 21:18-22). Size isn't strength.

The Lord rendered Absalom weak. Sometimes our strong point is the means of our downfall. No one was more handsome than Absalom. From the top of his head to the sole of his foot no blemish could be found in him. His hair was his crowning glory. When cut it weighed six pounds. One day in battle his hair caught in an oak tree, leaving him dangling, a perfect target for Joab, who thrust three darts through his heart (2 Sam. 14:25-26; 18:9-14).

The Lord can pierce a bravado facade. Dr. Tournier tells of two operations on the same morning. The first patient, a seemingly strong man, quipped flippantly as he was wheeled into the operating room, "Well, it's me for the slab today!" (meaning the morgue) The second patient was a weak, emotionally unstable woman. But she had faith and was honest enough to confess her fear of the operation and to pray to be set free from it. Under the anesthesia things were opposite. The man was restless, but the woman was calm and silent. In his facade of bravado, the strong man's artificial edifice crumbled.

The Lord can render strong animals weak. For entertainment one evening, passengers on a Mediterranean cruise were asked to write a brief essay on some aspect of the elephant. A Frenchman wrote on the love life of the elephant. A German passenger discussed the development of the elephant's tusk. An American wrote on the theme "Bigger Elephants." Yet, as he could have pointed out, size isn't everything. Bigger and stronger animals can be conquered by weak creatures A traveler in Africa and his guide came upon an incapacitated tiger. Jiggers, tiny insects no larger than a flea, had burrowed under the skin of the tiger's paw, which had swollen so badly that the animal could not defend itself.

The Lord can render strong leaders weak. Alexander the Great and Napoleon Bonaparte were doubtless two of the most powerful men of all time. Alexander sat on his throne like the lord of all creation, forcing all who approached to prostrate themselves at his feet. No power seemed capable of resisting his armies which conquered much of the known world. But he died in weakness at the age of 33 of fever caused by battle wounds plus gross dissipation. Within a few years his vast empire was torn into pieces by quarreling successors, making him one of the shortest-lived powers ever known. On his march to India Alexander had couches made for his soldiers five cubits (7 1/2') long to impress his enemies with an overwhelming sense of the size of his men. (Was this why Og, king of Bashan, built a bedstead 9 cubits [13 1/2'] long and preserved it for posterity—to perpetuate a sense of his gigantic size? [Deut. 3:11] Yet he was defeated in battle.)

Napoleon Bonaparte, colossal egotist, dreamed only of fame, fortune, and power for himself. He crushed without mercy anyone who blocked his aspirations. When an adviser estimated that his projected Russian campaign might cost a million men, he replied cynically, "What are a million men to me?" For over a decade much of Europe scraped before him. But a sudden turn of events landed Napoleon an exile on lonely St. Helena Island. His boasted strength had crumbled in ruin with France never again to regain her old glory as a world power.

Chuck Colson recalls the strength he and others had in the pre-Watergate era:

Think of the power at our fingertips: a mere command from one of us could mobilize generals and cabinet officers, even armies; we could hire or fire personnel and manage billions in agency budgets. Think of the privileges: a call to the military aide's office would produce a limousine or jet airplane; the National Gallery delivered classic paintings to adorn our office walls; red-jacketed stewards stood in waiting to serve food and drink 24 hours a day; private phones appeared wherever we traveled; secret service men were always within sight—as many as we wanted (*Loving God*, Zondervan, p. 67).

Yet how quickly that power dissipated for the President's men!

STRENGTH MADE PERFECT IN WEAKNESS

Anne Kiemel Anderson, well-known speaker and author, says, "Jesus does not choose the BEST people for His service. There are thousands, I know, more deserving than I of all the opportunities He has brought my way. I have come to believe that He chooses the weak instruments to ensure that His power might be more fully manifested" (*I Gave God Time*, Tyndale, 1982, p. 139).

Despite the barrenness of Sarah and the impotence of Abraham, through the strength of God they had a son in their old age.

Though Moses was weak in speech, a stutterer and slow talker, God enabled him to confront Pharaoh time and time again with the demand, "Let my people go" (Ex. 4:10; 5:1).

God chose Gideon, insignificant and lowborn, to deliver the Israelites from the Midianites who had completely devastated them. Gideon protested, "How can I deliver Israel? Behold, my clan is the weakest in Manasseh, and I am the least in my family" (Jud. 6:15, RSV). Though Gideon spoke the truth, God chose to reveal His strength through Gideon's weakness, having already addressed him as "you mighty man of valor" (v. 12).

How weak Daniel was in the den of lions. But God's power closed their mouths.

In listing the great heroes of faith, the writer of Hebrews spoke of those who "out of weakness were made strong, waxed valiant in fight, turned to flight the armies of the aliens" (11:34).

The largest missionary organization entering China in the late 19th century, according to historian Kenneth Scott LaTourette, was the China Inland Mission. Without the backing of any denomination or powerful ecclesiastical body, with missionaries guaranteed no fixed income and without personal solicitation of funds or collections at meetings, no other group sent so many missionaries to China or were found in so many provinces. Founder Hudson Taylor, on whom the burden of the mission chiefly fell, was a semi-invalid during much of his adult life. His wife and one of his children died. Yet he persevered. When confined to bed for a year in 1874, a seeming loss of time in which he could have been drumming up interest in China by speaking in churches and conventions, Taylor had a large map of China placed at the foot of his bed. Day and night he prayed God to furnish money and workers to enter the unreached inland provinces. That year he asked specifically for 18 workers, in 1881 for 70, and in 1886 for 100. Always the quotas were filled, and the necessary money obtained. He taught the candidates Chinese from his bed.

A friend once said to him, "It must give you deep satisfaction to be chosen by God to start this vast enterprise." Taylor replied, "It seemed to me that God looked over the whole world to find a man who was weak enough to do His work, and when He at last found me, He said, 'He is weak enough—he'll do!'" He added, "All God's giants have been weak men who did great things for God because they reckoned on His being with them."

God's strength made perfect in the weakness of old age. God's strength in Caleb's old age enabled him to drive out the giants from the Promised Land. At 85 Caleb claimed his inheritance:

> I am as strong this day as I was in the day that Moses sent me: as my strength was then, even so is my strength now, for war, both to go out, and to come in. Now therefore give me this mountain, whereof the Lord spake in that day; for thou heardest in that day how the Anakims were there, and that the cities were great and fenced: if so be the Lord will be with me, then I shall be able to drive them out (Josh. 14:6-12).

God's strength made perfect in the weakness of childhood. When the chief priests and scribes were indignant because children shouted praises to Jesus in the temple on the day of the Triumphal Entry, Jesus replied, "Out of the mouth of babes and sucklings the Lord has perfected praise" (Matt. 21:15-16).

Jeremiah thought he could not speak for God because he was too young. The Lord answered, "Say not, I am a child, for thou shalt go to all that I send thee, and whatsoever I command thee thou shalt speak" (Jer. 1:6-7).

Robert Coles, a Harvard professor, told of his taking training in New Orleans in 1960 and finding the city aflame with racial violence. A federal judge had pressured New Orleans' all-white schools to admit black students. This was the first test of federal will to enforce the U.S. Supreme Court ruling to desegregate schools. On November 14 three black first-graders entered one school, and another black child, Ruby Bridges, started at another.

Outside the latter school at 2 P.M. one afternoon, Coles saw a mob of people standing and screaming. He asked what was happening. Someone answered, "She's coming out in half an hour." When he asked who, the reply was a barrage of foul language. Soon out came little Ruby, accompanied by federal marshals. The people started in, calling her all sorts of names, waving their fists, telling her they were going to kill her. She left safely in a car. No one else came out, for the school had been completely boycotted by the whites.

Interviewing Ruby and her parents, Coles learned that the little girl was sleeping and eating well, playing with her friends, reading, and never seemed too upset. As the situation dragged on for weeks and months, Coles visited the teacher who saw Ruby by herself every day in the classroom. Said the teacher, "I don't understand this child. She seems so happy. She comes here so cheerfully." She told of Ruby walking through those crowds day by day—at least 50 angry people—every morning and afternoon. Coles admitted he was puzzled too. He couldn't help contrasting the calm reaction of Ruby and her family with the way well-to-do middle-class families in Boston behaved when their children, all white, had various difficulties.

One day the teacher told Coles that she saw Ruby talking with those people on the street that morning. Coles asked Ruby what she was saying to them. She replied, "I wasn't saying anything. I was just saying a prayer for them." Coles learned that Ruby prayed for them every night because she had been told in Sunday School to pray for those people, and because she heard her pastor pray every Sunday for them publicly.

At that point Coles did a little wondering. Would he have the fortitude to enter the Harvard Faculty Club if to do so he had to pass through hostile mobs twice a day without police protection. (Ruby had no police protection; that's why the U.S. marshals accompanied her.) He thought, "I'm sure I wouldn't pray for them."

Yet there was little Ruby, a mere child, who hadn't read any books on moral behavior, yet somehow for over a year, every school day, walking through mobs, praying for those people, and quoting Jesus' prayer, "Father, forgive them, for they know not what they do." Psychiatrist Coles summed up his puzzlement: "What does this leave us with now? The great paradox that Christ reminded us about is that sometimes those who are lonely and hurt and vulnerable—meek, to use the word—are touched by grace and can show the most extraordinary kind of dignity, and in that sense, inherit not only the next world, but even at times moments of this one. We who have so much knowledge and money and power look on confused, trying to mobilize the intellect, to figure things out. It is not so figurable, is it? These things are mysteries."

God's strength made perfect in the weakness of the body. A man, stricken with polio, dictated the following from an iron lung: "If by means of sickness a man can learn his own weakness and dependence upon God, that sickness has been a blessing. If sickness can teach a man that life is more than physical, and character more important than the body, then sickness has been a blessing. If sickness can prepare a man to serve others better, then sickness has been a blessing."

In an interview in *Leadership* magazine, Charles Farr, a minister in Denver's Church of the Epiphany, was asked what danger must be avoided in a healing ministry, for which his church is known. He replied:

> The notion that everything is always going to be successful—the Pollyanna, Prince Charming, happily-ever-after syndrome. There is no allowance for death or the realities of life. That's hard to square with a child born malformed or a quadriplegic like Joni Eareckson. Some people would say she hasn't 'named and claimed it,' or her faith isn't strong enough, or there is some sin in her life. But perhaps God has left her as she is to show that His strength is made perfect in weakness (spring quarter, 1985, p. 15).

Why didn't God remove Paul's thorn in the flesh despite Paul's three-time plea for its removal? The Lord explained, "My grace is sufficient for thee, for My strength is made perfect in weakness." Paul reacted submissively: "Most gladly therefore will I rather glory in my infirmities, that the power of Christ may rest upon me. Therefore I take pleasure in infirmities, in reproaches, in necessities, in persecutions, in distresses for Christ's sake, for when I am weak, then am I strong" (2 Cor. 12:7-10).

The Rev. Steve Harris, a New England pastor, became the father of a baby boy in 1980 born with the congenital defect commonly called spina bifida. In his first five years, the child underwent a dozen major operations, at least half of them life-threatening, and spent nearly a third of his life in hospital intensive-care units fighting for his life. Pastor Harris and his wife went through a long period of grief, hurt, and pain, making it difficult for him to function in the role of a spiritual leader. He asks:

Can hurting pastors—in need of ministry themselves—continue to be effective? My answer is yes. I've seen it happen. I've had to minister out of real weakness, but I've seen our church grow—in its ability to love, in its own gifts and talents (because the pastor isn't always available), and most important, we've grown in our trust in Jesus Christ, the Lord of His church (*Leadership*, spring quarter, 1985, p. 113).

The famous songwriter Fanny Crosby wrote more than 8,000 songs. When only six weeks of age, she suffered a minor eye inflammation which through a doctor's careless treatment left her permanently blind. She harbored no bitterness against the physician. To the contrary, she once said, "If I could meet him now, I would say thank you over and over again for making me blind." She felt her blindness was a gift from God to help her write the hymns that flowed from her pen.

A frail woman clutched the lectern of her home church one Sunday in 1963. "I'm on my way to Ghana in West Africa. I want to see if two Scriptures are true—'Without

Me ye can do nothing' (John 15:5) and 'I can do all things through Christ which strengtheneth me' " (Phil. 4:13). Aiming to translate the Scriptures into the language of the Vagla people, a tightly knit community of 7,000 who lived in 13 villages scattered over a 50-mile area, Marj Crouch found no interest among them in learning to read their language. She came home from her first term weak, both emotionally and physically. She already had rheumatoid arthritis. Pain constantly nagged her. Several operations loomed before her, making it easy to doubt God's purposes for her life.

When she left the second time for Ghana, she told the congregation, "I now realize how helpless I am in myself. But I'm glad to go back to the Vaglas for this reason: if anything remarkable happens among them, everyone will know that God did it."

Back in Ghana, suddenly her language helper, feeling concern for his own people, gathered together the chiefs and elders and urged them to learn their language. Also, another Wycliffe literacy specialist came to teach the Vaglas to read. A program of literacy took hold, especially during the six months of the dry season when the bored Vaglas were looking for something to do. The demand for classes could hardly be met.

During this time Marj faced struggles as arthritis advanced through her body. Out of her weakness God brought to pass a great accomplishment. On August 1, 1978 the Vagla people received the first printed copies of their New Testament. Marj comments, "As I look at the ups and downs on the graph of my life, I can see the peaks of achievement have always been produced in periods of great weakness." Fittingly, her story appeared in an article titled, "Strength Out of Weakness" in Wycliffe Bible Translators' publication, *In Other Words* (March 1985).

The source of God's strength. "Our sufficiency is of God" (2 Cor. 3:5), declared Paul. The psalmist said, "Power belongeth unto God" (62:11). Isaiah points out that the

Everlasting God never faints nor grows weary, but gives power to the faint, increasing the strength of those who have no might. Thus, those who wait upon the Lord renew their strength (40:28-29). Paul bids us be strong in the Lord, and in the strength of His might (Eph. 6:10). He prays that we be strengthened with all power according to His glorious might (Col. 1:11). Paul said he was able to do all things through the empowerment of Christ (Phil. 4:13). Peter says divine power has been granted to us in all things that pertain to godliness (2 Peter 1:3). Dr. J.C. Macaulay wrote that "one of the ablest evangelists today was advised as a young man by his faithful pastor not to try to be a preacher, as he had neither the gift nor presence for it. Also, no one would have suspected the untutored Boston shoe clerk (Moody) of becoming the century's greatest evangelist, whose name should be a household word in evangelical circles for generations to come" (*Epistle to the Hebrews*, Eerdmans, p. 281).

Satan tempted Jesus to exercise His power by turning stones into bread, receiving dominion over all the world, and by floating down ostentatiously from the temple pinnacle. But Jesus refused to display power to win followers. Instead, He emptied Himself of power, and chose to win from a posture of weakness, even the death of the cross. He was born in weakness and died in weakness, yet through that weakness His power has been displayed through the centuries.

Often what we think a failure in our Christian service turns out to be used of God. Dr. Paul Tournier recalls giving many lectures which drew hearty applause yet bore no fruit. But once, when invited to speak at a university, he felt right from the start that he was failing to make contact with his audience. A growing nervousness seized him. He clung to his notes which he could barely read, and laboriously recited what he had to say. He finished in a cold sweat. As the audience dispersed, Tournier could see his friends leaving quickly, too embarrassed to meet him.

On the way home in his car with his wife, he burst into tears.

But the next day he had a phone call from one of the university professors, confessing: "I've heard many first-class lectures in my life, and I've always come away from them arguing mentally with the speaker. I've never heard one as bad as yours last night, but I could not get to sleep afterward. It has raised a question in my mind—one that cannot be resolved by intellectual argument. May I come to see you?" Several weeks later that old professor underwent a conversion which has made them close friends, Dr. Tournier wrote (*The Strong and the Weak*, Westminster, p. 218).

Let us be careful not to boast in size or strength, realizing that in a moment God could trim us down to size, and make a grasshopper out of a supposed giant. Rather, let us realize the reality of our weakness, and rest in Him who delights to show His power through our infirmity.

TWELVE
REVERSED VERDICT

The first shall be last.
The last shall be first.

ana Corporation, maker of automobile and truck parts, vaulted from relative obscurity to the number two position in return on total capital among the *Fortune* 500 companies for the entire decade of the 1970s. Ren McPherson, former chairman of Dana who engineered this turnabout, followed this simple but revolutionary philosophy, "Turn the company back over to the people who do the work." His concept was expressed in his organizational "upside-down" chart. On top were the people on the production line; at the bottom was the chairman of the board. McPherson insisted that his chart was right side up. It was the others who were upside down.

Describing the chart, he said, "I draw it from the most important people down to the least important people. It's as simple as that." He saturated the annual report with pictures of people on the production line with their names. He commented, "Nobody ever spells the chairman's name wrong, or forgets to put his name under his picture. But what about the people who make him famous!"

Dana Corporation is not alone in the last-shall-be-first

philosophy for business success. A scattering of other companies have drawn their chart upside down, all of them with superior records, including Scandinavian Air System. The SAS chart is credited with turning the company around during the severe 1981-83 recession from an annual loss of $10 million to a profit of $70 million a year. Its chart consists of only three blocks. The top block is labeled "Customers." The middle block right below reads "First-line people who serve the customers." Then after a sizable gap comes a tiny bottom box labeled "Other," which stands for Accounting and Personnel Departments plus vice-presidents and managing director.

THE FIRST SHALL BE LAST

More than once Jesus suggested an upside-down chart for His kingdom. He put it, "But many that are first shall be last; and the last shall be first" (Matt. 19:30; also 20:16; Mark 10:31). His elevation of childhood was a reversal of the usual. One day when His disciples were arguing over who was the greatest in the kingdom, Jesus placed a little child in their midst and gave an object lesson. In the natural order of things, we would have expected Jesus to say to the child, "Now you grow up and be like Peter, James, John, and the other disciples." Instead, Jesus told Peter, James, John, and the other disciples to be like the little child: "Except ye be converted, and become as little children, ye shall not enter into the kingdom of heaven. Whosoever therefore shall humble himself as this little child, the same is greatest in the kingdom of heaven" (Matt. 18:3-4).

Jesus did not mean that children are born saints, but rather that, as yet uncorrupted by adult customs, they possess many qualities which constitute true greatness. Childlikeness, not childishness, sums up characteristics the Lord wants His followers to possess. For example, unlike adults, children are not afraid to ask questions. Adult pretense could learn a few lessons from children's openness, frankness, and guilelessness. Children forgive easily whereas hurt adult vanity often leads to grudge-holding for years. To be converted, adults need childlike humility to overcome their pride, admit their lack of righteousness, and confess their need of Christ. By upholding childhood, Jesus made the last first, and the first last.

Power can be easily reversed. Ilse Koch, married to the commandant of Buchenwald concentration camp, earned the title of "Witch of Buchenwald" through her atrocities on inmates during World War II. Her husband was shot by German troops the day before Allied forces occupied Buchenwald. Her power was stripped from her. She was sentenced to life in prison at hard labor by an Allied war crimes court in 1947 which heard witnesses tell how Ilse Koch had lampshades and handbags made out of prisoners' skins. When I read a few years ago that she hanged herself in jail, I thought how positions had been reversed. She was gone, while many prisoners lived who had been able to confront her in court. The first became last, and the last first.

In a visit to Dachau concentration camp, I saw not only the crematory, but also the barracks where hundreds of prisoners were crowded, including the location where Bishop Niemoller was detained. During Niemoller's incarceration, Hitler raged and roared over much of Europe. But soon the tables were turned. Hitler committed suicide, and Niemoller was restored to his position.

Joseph's brothers threw "the dreamer" into a pit, then cruelly sold him into slavery. They held the upper hand by sheer numbers, age, and experience. About two decades later the brothers bowed with faces to the ground before Joseph. They didn't realize that this second-in-command of all Egypt was their brother, whom they had treated so shabbily. When he revealed his identity, they were terrified. Again, reversal of power.

Proverbs speaks of a slave who, handling himself wisely, comes to rule over a son who acts disgracefully and to share in the family inheritance (17:2).

Haman, avid anti-Semitic prime minister over the ancient Persian Empire, concocted a plot to replenish the king's treasuries by extermination of the Jews and confiscation of their property on an appointed day. Unable to wait for that day to get rid of Mordecai, a Jewish servant in the royal palace who would not bow to him, Haman built gallows and entered the king's presence for permission to hang Mordecai thereon. Haman's strategy backfired. He was ordered to set Mordecai on the king's horse, put the king's robe and crown on him, and lead him through the streets. How the populace must have laughed, for they knew full well Haman's hatred of Mordecai, as Moredcai sat astride the royal horse, regally arrayed, and Haman walked below, announcing with words that must have choked in his throat, "This is the man the king delights to honor." A few hours later Haman was hanged on his own gallows and Mordecai was named prime minister in Haman's place. Another reversal of power.

The Sanhedrin had the power to condemn the Lord Jesus. But the stone which the builders rejected became the chief cornerstone, while the Sanhedrin faded into oblivion (1 Peter 2:7).

The late Dr. Walter Maier of the radio "Lutheran Hour" related a short piece of fiction in which he imagined Pilate's life after he was deposed from office and banished to exile. An old friend who had been with Pilate in Jerusalem asked, "Do you remember the young Galilean you had crucified during the Passover one year—Jesus of Nazareth?" Pilate looked blankly out into the waters of the Mediterranean. Slowly rubbing his head, as if to awaken dead memories, finally he answered, "Jesus! Jesus of Nazareth? I cannot recall Him." Though forgetting that Jesus stood before his tribunal, someday Pilate will stand before the tribunal of Christ the Judge.

The wicked who prosper someday will find things reversed. People ask repeatedly, "Why do the wicked prosper, and the godly suffer? Why do bad things happen to good people?" Perhaps the upside-down principle of the first last, and the last first, provides a partial answer. The wicked rich, well-fed, prosperous, seem to be top-dog now. The godly poor, hungry, barely eking out an existence, seem today's underdog. But Jesus spoke of a day when wrongs will be righted, and things put in proper perspective. He promised that to those who suffer for His sake: "Blessed are ye that hunger now, for ye shall be filled. Blessed are ye that weep now, for ye shall laugh. Blessed are ye, when men shall hate you, and when they shall separate you from their company, and shall reproach you, and cast out your names as evil, for the Son of man's sake. Rejoice ye in that day, and leap for joy, for, behold, your reward is great in heaven." Then He warned, "But woe unto you that are rich! For ye have received your consolation. Woe unto you that are full! For ye shall hunger. Woe unto you that laugh now! For ye shall mourn and weep" (Luke 6:21-25). In *The Divine Comedy* Dante placed Cleopatra, Helen of Troy, and a host of emperors, kings, great generals, and even many religious leaders in hell.

One's status can be reversed. Dying Jacob, in blessing the sons of Joseph, did a strange thing. He crossed his hands, placing the right hand of blessing on the younger Ephraim, and his left on the older Manasseh. Thinking his father's failing eyesight the cause of this switching, the displeased Joseph reversed Jacob's hands, pointing out the supposed mistake. But Jacob declared that neither ignorance nor misunderstanding had inverted the blessing. He had guided his hands deliberately, declaring that though the older would become a great people, the younger would be greater (Gen. 48:8-20). The tribe of Ephraim did prove to be greater; in fact the ten northern tribes were often referred to as Ephraim.

The preference of the younger over the older is a principle running through Scripture. Cain is rejected; Abel is honored. Ishmael is exiled; Isaac is heir. Esau is hated;

Jacob is loved. Reuben is displaced by Joseph. Manasseh is exceeded by Ephraim. Aaron may be older, but it's Moses who is the emancipator. Not firstborn Eliab, nor the next six, but the youngest, David, was anointed king over Israel. The Old Covenant gives way to the New. In the first Adam all sin, stand condemned, and sentenced to death. In the second Adam we are declared righteous, and given life.

The order of nature gives way to the order of grace. On the natural side, older sons had the right to receive the blessing. But the younger was often blessed above the older, lest grace should be confounded with nature, overcoming the impression that natural effects could never be changed by grace, or that grace would have to wait on nature. The younger receiving the blessing shows that, in God's sovereign economy, what seems inferior by nature can be made superior by grace.

To put it another way, the firstborn had no special claim on God's mercy. Nor does native intelligence, nor business acumen, nor social position, nor higher education, nor sweet disposition, nor excellent character. God looks not on the outward man, brains, brawn or beauty, book knowledge, or government bonds. God can work in a heart to overcome deficiency of natural talents.

The motley gang that followed David in exile consisted of the distressed, debtors, and discontented. But this band of malcontents became the nucleus of David's leadership (1 Sam. 22:2; 27:2).

God's finest servants haven't always been the most eligible. The 12 Apostles had little to commend them for His choice of followers. Several were fishermen. Philip appeared indecisive. Peter was impulsive. James and John were hotheads. Thomas radiated cynicism. Matthew was considered a traitor to his country. Zealot Simon was a dangerous revolutionary. Some of the women who ministered to Jesus had shady reputations. The Apostle Paul seems to have made an unimposing appearance, short, weak, and afflicted with an eye disease.

Most of God's servants seem not to have been rich, nor highly educated, or among the upper 400. God can and does use people with high IQs and material wealth, but lack of such does not disqualify one from His favor or service. Giving a rich man the best seat because he is bejewelled and well-clothed, and giving a poor man an inferior seat because he lacks such things is not God's way.

Fame is fickle. In April 1985 star baseball pitcher Denny McLain of the late '60s received a sentence of 23 years in federal prison. For several years he had smoked his fastball past hitters for the Detroit Tigers. At the height of his career, when just 24 in 1968, he won 31 games, the first pitcher since Dizzy Dean to win 30 games, and so far the last to do so. After he won his second Cy Young Award as the best pitcher in the American League in 1969 with 24 victories, his world began to collapse. Suspended temporarily from baseball in 1970 for running an informal bookmaking operation in the Tigers' clubhouse, he was traded to Washington and lost 22 games in 1971, then disappeared forever from the major leagues, finished at the age of 28. In the years following till his sentencing at age 41, he twice declared bankruptcy, got involved in numerous businesses, and then in March 1984 was arrested on charges of racketeering, extortion, and drug trafficking. In a prepared statement, McLain read in court, "I don't know how you get to where I was today from where I was 17 years ago." But he did admit he suffered from avarice and bad judgment in trying to make a fast buck. *The New York Times* sports article about McLain was titled "A King No Longer" (April 27, 1985).

Yes, fame fades fast. How many TV programs in the top ten a dozen years ago are on the air now or even remembered? The name of British statesman Neville Chamberlain was known to almost every Westerner during the crucial days just prior to World War II, especially when Germany invaded Poland in 1939. Yet within two years he had died and was practically forgotten, perhaps unknown to most readers of this book. After a celebrity's death, someone wrote, "He died two months ago and is not forgotten yet. Then there's hope a man's memory may outlive his life by half a year."

Many secretly desire to perpetuate their names, perhaps perform some feat that will bring lasting recognition. But anyone who performs a task to win lasting fame is usually doomed to failure. Because men wished to make a name for themselves, they built the tower of Babel. But who can name just one of the builders? Their names perished with the tower.

The question comes—what kind of labor lives on? The answer—only as men and women come in vital contact with God through Jesus Christ, and link themselves in dedication to His eternal program, so that their labor is in harmony with His divine will. Who can name a Pharisee who rejected Christ? Who cannot name a disciple who revered Him? Who can name the man who swung the ax that beheaded the Apostle Paul. Who in the Christian world has not heard of that prince of apostles? Of course, in common grace some men achieve a measure of fame for some outstanding achievement, but in the light of eternity it will fade, unless related to Christ's program and glory.

Famous baseball slugger Babe Ruth reportedly said: "Most of the people who have really counted in my life were not famous. Nobody ever heard of them, except those who knew and loved them. I knew an old minister once. His hair was white; his face shone. I have written my name on thousands of baseballs in my life. The old minister wrote his name on just a few simple hearts. How I envy him. He was not trying to please his own immortal soul. So fame never came to him. I am listed as a famous home-runner, yet beside that obscure minister, who was so good and so wise, I never got to first base."

Sometimes the privileged lose out to the deprived. A book

published soon after World War II titled *They Found the Church There* tells how enlightened American soldiers and sailors found real Christians in the most unlikely "heathen" places such as the South Sea Islands. Marooned on a supposedly cannibal island, American sailors on cautious patrol came across a group of natives singing hymn tunes. Later contact revealed that these natives were Christians, won by missionaries. On a Japanese-controlled island, American airmen, forced down when their plane malfunctioned, were discovered by natives who covertly brought them food day after day till the war ended. The airmen learned that missionaries had preceded them, and won to Christ these folk who now displayed their Christian love to the airmen. In fact, the book tells how many American servicemen were won to Christ through the testimony of such natives. What a switch—Americans from a country where the Gospel is preached in most every town and proclaimed by TV and radio coast to coast evangelized by jungle natives just a few years removed from heathenism and cannibalism! The sad truth is that millions of privileged Americans are still outside the Rock of Ages, whereas millions of outsiders, former heathen in many parts of the world, have come under the Shadow of the Almighty. They tell us that in a few years Africa will be more Christian than the U.S.

Something like this happened to God's privileged people. Many in Jesus' day thought that tracing their genealogy to Abraham brought an automatic ticket to salvation. But Jesus warned that in a coming day many claiming the patriarch as their father would be excluded from the kingdom. Even though they pled, "We have eaten and drunk in Thy presence, and Thou hast taught in our streets," He would reply, "I know you not whence ye are; depart from Me, all ye workers of iniquity." Then the unprivileged would come from the east, and from the west, and from the north, and from the south, and would sit down in the kingdom of God along with Abraham, and

Isaac, and Jacob, and all the prophets. "And, behold, there are last which shall be first, and there are first which shall be last" (Luke 13:26-30). It's not enough to enjoy the association of a Christian family, church, or country, and remain just an observer. We must personally appropriate the gift of the Gospel to our own lives.

The self-righteous have an unpleasant surprise coming. Jesus told the self-righteous leaders a parable of two sons ordered by their father to work in his vineyard. One refused but later changed his mind and went to work. The other agreed to work, but failed to follow through. Jesus pointed out that the one who did the father's bidding, though at first rebelling, was the obedient son. Then Jesus drove home His point, "That the publicans and the harlots go into the kingdom of God before you" (Matt. 21:28-31).

The woman caught in adultery found Jesus' pardon while the Pharisee Simon, Jesus' host, missed it. Jesus forgave the woman, but the scribes and Pharisees who talked about stoning her drifted off unforgiven. When the Pharisee and the publican went up to the temple to pray, the Pharisee went to his house still guilty, for he had not sought mercy, whereas the publican, crying out in his need, went home justified (Luke 18:10-14). Jesus' ministry appealed to the lowest, least, and last.

The prodigal son, on his repentant return, enjoyed the fatted calf, ringed finger, and best robe, whereas his older brother, so good and so moral, but so unloving and out of tune with his father, sulked out into the night, moping and missing the festivities celebrating his wayward brother's homecoming.

THE LAST SHALL BE FIRST

When the rich young ruler turned away from Jesus because he was unwilling to surrender his wealth, Peter asked Jesus, "We've left everything to follow You. What do we get out of it?" Without rebuke for this seemingly commercial question, Jesus replied, "Everyone that hath forsaken houses, or brethren, or sisters, or father, or mother, or wife, or children, or land for My name's sake shall receive an hundredfold, and shall inherit everlasting life" (Matt. 19:29). Then Jesus added, "But many that are first shall be last, and the last shall be first" (v. 30).

Giving down here reevaluated up there. An earlier chapter points out that many rich of this earth will be poor up there, and many poor down here will be rich up there. A rich woman who lived in a magnificent mansion dreamed she had died and in heaven an angel was directing her to her new home. He took her down a street with its row of lovely mansions, then down another with its not so lavish homes. "Which mansion is it?" she asked. The angel silently continued leading her to a row of regular houses, then to dilapidated shacks, one of which he indicated was hers, explaining to the horror-stricken woman, "We did the best we could with the material you sent up."

C.T. Studd, all-England cricketeer who became a missionary on three continents, inherited the equivalent of $125,000 on his 25th birthday. Contributing most of it to missionary organizations, he gave the rest to his wife as a wedding present. Not to be outdone, she gave it all away for Christian purposes. Their financial rating may have tumbled down here, but it skyrocketed up in heaven.

Dr. Roy Gustafson, a member of the Billy Graham team, tells of visiting Zaire and seeing an old, bent woman coming with her offering. "In a good week," the missionaries estimated, "she can earn the equivalent of a dollar. She's the biggest giver in this church." Though known practically to no one on earth, she is well-known to God.

A church treasurer read off the gifts contributed by members the past year. "Mr. A., $2,000; Mr. B., $1,500." Loud clapping followed the reading of each amount. Then he read, "Widow C., $500." Absolute silence. Then the chairman remarked, "Methinks I hear the clapping of pierced hands."

When the selfish rich man dies, he leaves his riches.

When the sacrificial poor man dies, he goes to his riches.

Service will be reappraised. Immediately following the dialogue with Peter about rewards, the next chapter in Matthew tells the story of the landowner who went out early in the morning to hire workers (Matt. 20:1-16). Those who started early agreed to work for one denarius for the day. Other workers began at noon, some at 3, and some as late as 5 o'clock, just an hour before the end of the workday. When they lined up for their pay, surprisingly they all received the same wage, one denarius. Naturally the early birds complained, "You haven't checked the time cards. You've given the 5 o'clock starters, who worked just one hour, the same amount as those of us who've worked a full day!" The landowner reminded them of their wage agreement, and of his right to do what he wanted with his own money.

The parable teaches that seniority in the kingdom does not mean superiority. It's not how long we have served, but how faithfully. Christians who are converted late in life or who die young, if rewarded on the basis of the number of years of service, wouldn't stand a chance to be rewarded like veteran servants. But it's not quantity, but quality that counts with the Lord. It's possible to serve long years with improper motive, and receive little reward. It's also possible for latecomers, who thought they had ruined their lives but who serve their few remaining years faithfully, to be rewarded richly. Jesus ended the parable with this principle, "So the last shall be first, and the first last" (v. 16).

In the day of judgment believers may discover that supposed deeds of greatness will turn out to be wood, hay, and stubble. Conversely, the little acts we deemed of no significance, giving a cup of cold water in His name, God will acknowledge as gold, silver, and precious stones.

How well I remember Joe Killigrew, superintendent of the Jerry McAuley Cremorne Mission near Times Square, New York, where I took our young people regularly to help in services. He was saved out of alcoholism at 47, and two years later to the very day was appointed superintendent. He lived only till 54. Regretting his wasted years, he devoted himself wholeheartedly to winning lost men and women to Christ in his remaining time on earth. At his funeral I heard it announced that 9,000 men had come to Christ during his ministry there. Will not his reward be greater than many who served a whole lifetime?

The faithful unsung will be honored. Many counted among the Christians' *Who's Who* down here will not be listed in the heavenly *Who's Who.* Some faithful crossroads pastor may even outshine Spurgeon up there, and some unsung missionary outglow the famous Livingstone. Some who sit here on pulpit chairs will likely fade into the background, while quiet, faithful pew-sitters get top spots. Many high on the totem pole of Christian organizations will have lower status.

A legend centers around a contest announced at the start of a church building. On completion of the construction, an angel would award a prize to the person who made the most significant contribution to the finished project. Who would win—the architect, the contractor, the craftsman in glass, the sculptor of lovely statuary, or the carpenter assigned the fancy woodwork? All worked hard. What a surprise when the recipient proved to be an elderly peasant woman who every day carried hay to the ox that pulled the stones for the stonecutters!

Someday Jesus' "Well done" will fall on the ears of many whom the world dubs failures, while bypassing many lauded as successful.

Jesus invites us to an amazing upside-down kingdom, where down is up, where slow is fast, where to give up is to gain, where you die in order to live, where little is much and the weak are strong, where you can have joy in the midst of misery, where becoming a slave you find freedom, where following the foolishness of God you become wise, where the last are first.

HOLY CONTRADICTIONS

Say that up is down,
Declare that rich is poor,
Argue that gain is loss,
and I will ask
if last is first.

Preach that grief is joy,
Insist that fools are wise,
Prove that death is life,
and I will believe
that last is first.

—BARBARA ESCH SHISLER